The
Essential
College

PRESS

The Essential College
Copyright © 2006 Bruce Haywood
All rights reserved

ISBN 978-1-880977-16-3

Published by XOXOX Press 2006

XOXOX Press
102 Gaskin Avenue, Box 51
Gambier, OH 43022

website **http://xoxoxpress.com**
email **books@xoxoxpress.com**

Printed by Printing Arts Press, Mt. Vernon, Ohio
Editorial assistance by Susan Church
Book design by Jerry Kelly
Printed in USA

Library of Congress Cataloging-in-Publication Data

Haywood, Bruce.
  The essential college / by Bruce Haywood.
    p. cm.
  ISBN-13: 978-1-880977-16-3
  1. Education, Humanistic--United States. 2. Education, Higher--United States--Philosophy. 3. Education--Aims and objectives--United States.   I. Title.
  LC1023.H39 2006
  378.012--dc22
                                          2005037197

The Essential College

Bruce Haywood

President Emeritus,
Monmouth College
Monmouth, Illinois

Former Dean and Provost,
Kenyon College
Gambier, Ohio

PRESS

Gambier, Ohio
2006

for Gretchen, always

	Preface *6*
I.	*A First Question* *9*
II.	*Opposite Poles* *30*
III.	*Visionary Leadership* *53*
IV.	*The Chalmers Kenyon* *74*
V.	*Leadership Lost* *94*
VI.	*Salvation in Old Ideas* *122*
VII.	*The Magic Mountain* *146*
VIII.	*Independent Contractors* *172*
IX.	*The Purpose of Knowing* *193*
X.	*The Liberal Arts Beleaguered* *211*
XI.	*The Once and Future College* *232*
XII.	*A Curriculum for the Essential College* . *252*
	Acknowledgements *265*

Preface

In the early spring of 2004, on a visit to Lake Forest, Illinois, I drove past the campus of a private college. It was like many another I had seen over the years: a few handsome brick buildings set among towering trees, trimmed lawns, a serene oasis in a bustling world. I slowed to look at the campus, sadly and more closely than I would otherwise have done, for I had read in the *Chicago Tribune* just a few days before that the college would close its doors forever at the end of the academic year. Neither its founding church nor its meager endowment was able any longer to keep it alive.

Because I have spent my professional life working for and with private colleges, the death of one comes close to being like the loss of a relative, personally affecting, a reminder of the weakened condition of others in the family. Colleges of that kind, often known only to their relatively few graduates (who yet have loved their alma mater passionately and gratefully) are increasingly threatened by the ever-growing system of public universities and community colleges, where tax dollars allow tuition and fees at a fraction of the rate the private colleges must charge.

But no less a threat to the private college exists in the fall from favor of liberal education. Once the accepted mode of American undergraduate education, in colleges and universities alike, the study of the liberal arts can today barely hold its own in institutions where the immediately practical, pre-professional studies take pride of place. Apart from a small number of very heavily endowed colleges, virtually every liberal arts college in the country must wonder whether it can survive the next fifty years in a society that seems less and less to understand its need for the college's work.

In the chapters that follow I shall describe the factors which have brought the liberal arts colleges to their present unhappy state, writing first, so as to put a human face on those developments, of my experience at Kenyon College, where for nearly thirty years I witnessed at first hand changes that mirror those at nearly all similar colleges in that period. My narrative will tell of my discovery, as an immigrant from England, of liberal education and that uniquely American institution, the liberal arts college.

Underlying all I write will be the question that I began to shape nearly sixty years ago, in the wreckage of Hitler's Germany: what is the relationship of education and morality? That question, central to my life, informs this book. It sets for me the poles of the amoral "pursuit of knowledge for its own sake," the mode of the contemporary American university, and the moral purpose of liberal education as I came to know it in my first years at Kenyon. I shall write of vision and leadership, as well as their absence, of the threat of financial disaster, of the struggle to maintain a traditional character in the face of radical changes and new assumptions about the purpose of higher education. Inevitably, some parts of my narrative will seem like a lament for something that has been lost, but I shall write finally of my hope that trustees, presidents and faculty members of some colleges can be convinced, while there is still time, that liberal education is so vital to the future of the Republic that they will seek to preserve in their institutions the essential college that has inspired so many generations of Americans to seek a purposeful life, rewarding to themselves and to their society.

Chapter I
A First Question

In the twenty-seven months I spent in Germany immediately after the end of the war in Europe, the terrifying facts of Hitler's twelve years in power came to light. The war crimes trials produced massive evidence of the evil of the Nazi regime; we were learning names like Buchenwald and Dachau to add to Rotterdam and Warsaw; films were shown around the world of the pitiful victims of the concentration camps; in the press there were ongoing accounts of pillage, rape, and murder. All of this horror had been wrought in the name of bringing into being a new order, a new world in which some would be masters and the rest would be slaves.

My work for both British and American intelligence in Bremerhaven put me face to face with Germans every day. I spent several evenings sitting in the movie theater with them, observing their reactions to the concentration camp films they were obliged to watch. In the first months I shipped down to Bremen every week at least a dozen Germans I had arrested because they were functionaries of the Nazi regime. Many of them protested that they were never really believers; they were just swept into their role by the circumstances of the time. Others, particularly members of the SS, were still arrogant in their faith, imagining that Nazism would have a second chance, another day. Some of the former office holders were eager not only to denounce Hitler, but also to denounce those in their community who were the "true" Nazis; they were useful informants, if less than attractive human beings.

One German I was soon to know face to face became for me the epitome of one aspect of Nazi evil. I first learned the name Werner Zacharias from the list of the war criminals that the Royal Air Force wished to capture; he was identified as a Bremerhaven resident. A Gestapo man, he was accused of having murdered thirty-eight British and Canadian airmen. Once he returned to the city, after being released from a POW camp in Denmark, I quickly informed the RAF investigators in Hamburg. Delighted by the news, they asked that we arrest him and hold him overnight until they could pick him up.

My American colleagues and I found Zacharias sitting comfortably by the stove in his in-laws' kitchen. He wasn't surprised that we wished to see him. He came along without resisting and readily answered questions that were put to him. But he balked when I told him he was charged with the murder of thirty-eight airmen. He insisted that we were misinformed. The correct figure was thirty-six.

A First Question

Calmly and without emotion he told us what he had done and why. North of Bremerhaven, where he had been stationed during the war, was the North Sea coast line which RAF and RCAF bombers crossed night after night on their way to Hamburg, Hannover, and other targets. The Germans had massed anti-aircraft batteries along the coast and there were fighter planes to attack the bombers as well. Inevitably planes were brought down and sometimes crewmen were able to parachute to temporary safety. They were quickly rounded up and turned over to the local police. It was Zacharias's job to go out with a driver to pick them up and bring them back to Bremerhaven for interrogation. The Gestapo records captured by the British troops who overran the Bremerhaven area recorded the fact that thirty-eight of them didn't make it, but two of them, Zacharias insisted, were dead of their wounds when they were handed over to him. The thirty-six he readily admitted murdering were killed with a bullet in the back of the head. On the way back to Bremerhaven he would stop the car and invite the captives to step out and have a cigarette. Then he executed them. And execution, he insisted, was appropriate, for were they not war criminals, the destroyers of German cities, the murderers of schoolchildren? Had they been tried in Bremerhaven, he claimed, they would have certainly been declared guilty and hanged. He was saving the state time and money.

I never found it difficult to understand men like Werner Zacharias. He was a thug, a thug in a uniform which gave him the power and authority to torture and kill in the name of his country. There were obviously many like him in Germany. There are many like him in every country; theirs is an evil that has to be restrained by the laws of a civilized society. I sent men like Zacharias to jail—and in his case eventual hanging in England—with no question in my mind about the rightness of their punishment.

In later months I found a very different kind of German sitting on the other side of my desk, one of the sophisticated supporters of the Nazi horror. There have been people, not all of them Germans, who have wished not to see any connection between the Zachariases and these others. The connection surely existed. The amoral ethos of German society in the Hitler years, when there was earnest, learned discussion of the value to the state of euthanizing handicapped children or of allowing only the "racially pure" to reproduce, was necessary for the Zachariases to emerge to authority and to commit the monstrous crimes of which they were guilty.

By the time I found myself interrogating Hitler's intelligentsia we had moved away from "automatic" arrests and were deep in the process that was called "de-Nazification." Members of the professions—white-collar workers, managers, technicians, all of whom had been required to join the Nazi Party in order to hold their positions—had to be screened and either certified for continuing practice or identified as unfit to serve. It was in questioning these people, particularly the teachers and pastors, that I began to shape the question that was to occupy my thinking for many a year: what brought educated men and women to embrace the immorality of Hitler's regime and to support the persecution of Jews, the takeover of territory, the war?

Some, it was soon clear to me, had so dreaded the possibility of a Communist victory in Germany in the chaotic nineteen-twenties that they had early come to believe in Hitler as their only defense. They were eager to join the Party back then, less eager to support it as its intentions became more apparent. Others had wished to remain "unpolitical"—how often did that word echo from my office walls!—and had joined only because they would otherwise have been destitute. But there were some who had been, I was gradually able to get from them, convinced supporters of Nazi doctrine in all its aspects: believers in the theory of the master race, believers in a Jewish conspiracy to destroy the West, believers in the righteousness of Hitler's teachings. And these men were the products of Germany's vaunted system of higher education. They enjoyed quoting Goethe and Schiller to me; they spoke proudly of Beethoven and Bach, of Kant and Hegel, of "the land of poets and thinkers" that was Germany in the nineteenth century. One such man told me that he was glad to see me in a British uniform; he had feared he would be questioned by Americans, "for they, you know, have no culture." By my standards of the time these men were extraordinarily well educated. Their embrace of Hitler's evil or denial of the evil I could not then begin to understand. My later reading brought me gradually to see the extent to which the years of their schooling and university study had made them receptive to Hitler's distorted view of morality.

The German universities won their reputation in and after the great age of revolution, an age with "liberty" on its lips, the age that saw far-reaching political change in North America and France, the beginnings of the industrial revolution in Britain, and in Germany an intellectual revolution to match the Renaissance. Many a historian has credited nineteenth-century Germany with creating the intellectual and artistic breakthroughs which have defined the modern age. The ferment that brought forth so much of modern science, modern philosophy, and the Romantic movement in the arts emerged in what had been regarded as the most backward place in Europe. "Germany" meant then scores of kingdoms, principalities, and dukedoms where some dialect of German was spoken and the German of Luther read. More of a common denominator was a medieval social system with brutal political repression. Friedrich Schiller did not dare publish an "Ode to Freedom"; instead he called his celebration of the indomitable human spirit an "Ode to Joy". The triumphant music of Beethoven's Ninth Symphony tells us that he understood the code. It was dangerous to speak or write of liberty.

It could be dangerous in the universities, too, where new ideas were pushing aside traditional notions and where inherited practices were being challenged. To protect themselves against the clerical and secular authorities who would have condemned them, university faculties declared themselves to be apart from their society. They let the walls of their studies and laboratories surround them and insisted that their pursuits had no extramural implications; they were engaged in the pursuit of knowledge for its own sake, in value-free inquiry. They focused their energies on limited topics of inquiry, seeking "the truth within the discipline." Thus secured and thus focused, German scholars made remarkable breakthroughs in virtually every sphere of intellectual activity: in philology, in history and archeology, in physics, chemistry, biology, geology, and eventually in new disciplines like sociology and psychology. There is scarcely a modern discipline that does not honor a German—and often a Jewish German—as its high priest.

Soon the reputation of German scholars, working single-mindedly at their research, spread to this country, where Goethe's fame had preceded theirs. Regard for German achievements was high, first among American thinkers like Emerson and then in our schools and colleges. A remarkably large number of Americans journeyed across the Atlantic to study with the German masters, bringing back with them stories of German accomplishment and urging the imitation of German practice in focusing upon a limited field of inquiry. It seems not to have been apparent to those who spoke admiringly of German achievement that German intellectual life was marked by separation from the social and political. Neither do they seem to have been aware of dangerous undercurrents in German thought, most particularly in the philosophy of Friedrich Nietzsche, whose voice, by the century's closing decade, was the most powerful voice in the German academy.

A First Question

Those who admire Nietzsche's writings have sought to exonerate him of all charges that his philosophy influenced Hitler. It is no difficult task for them to bring us to believe that Hitler was not capable of appreciating the subtleties of Nietzsche's thinking. But they cannot explain away the enormous influence Nietzsche had on generations of those who passed through the universities. Besides, there are disturbing parallels between Hitler's theories of master and slave peoples and Nietzsche's preachings on morality. In his famous essay "Beyond Good and Evil" Nietzsche argues that "good" and "evil" are necessary concepts for the masses of people, who are incapable of truly independent thought. A society will need such concepts to preserve order and civility; the common folk can be taught them in their churches and schools. But the independent thinker will wish to be free of such limiting notions. He will advance "beyond" them and create his own notions of what is permitted him and what is not. In a sometimes popularized and vulgarized form, Nietzsche's philosophy swept the universities where "good" and "evil" had already been set outside the walls. How seductive it was for young men to think themselves the masters, how easy to be contemptuous of the ignorant masses who had to be led by the nose.

The Essential College

I have long since rejected the oft-asserted argument that Hitler corrupted the universities and forced himself upon their faculties. Those faculties proved, in the main, quite eager to expel their Jewish colleagues and to support Hitler in every way they could. And not just the scientists, architects, and physicians, whose work for the Nazis has come under scrutiny. Their colleagues in the humanities had created acceptance of amorality in intellectual life; it was but a step to denying a moral dimension to political and social questions. The universities had prepared the ground for the seed Hitler sowed across Germany. They formed the vanguard for the idea of a German "mission."

The German idea of amoral inquiry—investigation separated from a context and not limited by an ethical system—was made admirable by being called "the pursuit of knowledge for its own sake." It found its first beachhead in this country with the creation of Johns Hopkins University. The founders of that institution could have imagined neither what the consequences of their well-intended actions would be, nor that Johns Hopkins would become the model for every university in this country. They seem to have confidently believed that students, having been liberally educated in the undergraduate college, would contain the value-free inquiry that was intended for the graduate school within their system of morality. The founders could not foresee that the graduate schools would eventually so dominate the universities that their modes of inquiry, their practice of isolating questions from larger contexts, their amorality itself, would push down into the undergraduate division and destroy the ruling idea of the American college.

The American college was founded to be a moral institution, to bring its students to choose the good and to act on it. Virtually every college and university existing in this country before the middle decades of the nineteenth century was a church foundation. Very few Americans today know that Princeton was first a Presbyterian college; even fewer, that the University of Michigan was similarly a Presbyterian foundation. Meant in the first instance to be the training ground for future ministers of the denomination, such colleges at once attracted parents who were ambitious to see their children educated to become leaders in their community. There was never a year in the history of Yale College when prospective ministers outnumbered other students, and such enrollments were characteristic everywhere. Thomas Jefferson had provided a great impulse to the development of a college system when he called on higher education to prepare those who would preserve the Republic. In countless older college catalogues, echoes can be found of Jefferson's belief that the nation's leaders must be liberally educated men who would provide their fellows with a sustaining vision of the better society.

We can chart the movement of the western frontier by noting the founding dates of colleges across the Middle West, so many of them in Ohio that we used to joke that every town with more than four intersections had a college. A reading of their mission statements tells us that they were there not to train their students in useful, marketable skills, but to educate them to an understanding of their humanity and their responsibility to their world. A characteristic statement of such purpose can be found in the 1955 Catalogue of Monmouth College, where I served as President from 1980 to 1994; it is explicit in proposing a moral liberal education: "Monmouth College proposes to provide young men and women with the understanding of the world in which they live .... To provide them with an intelligent understanding and comprehension of the basic structure of the world of physical nature, the world of living organisms from the lowest to the highest forms, the world of human society and institutions, the world of ideas including the products of both imagination and

conceptual thinking, and the world of values ....
Monmouth affirms that such a course of study is
the only sound foundation for an effective life in
modern society, both as a necessary preparation
for further training in any occupation or
profession that involves the exercise of personal
responsibility, and for any function in any phase of
human life requiring judgment and understanding
in addition to mere skill."

We must not overlook in that text, among the
readily recognizable identities of sciences, social
sciences, and humanities, the reference to the
"world of values," with its clear assumption that
values can be proposed and examined just as
earnestly and as rigorously as any other object of
study. It is an essential antecedent to the sentence
which argues that liberal education is the "only
sound foundation for an effective life." Such belief
was shared by all American colleges before World
War II; it continued to shape the mission statements
of colleges for decades after the war, often long
after a college was no longer recognizable, in its
practice, as a liberal arts college.

In the dozen years that I was a member of
the national board of consultants of the National
Endowment for the Humanities, I studied the
catalogues of a score of client colleges, seeking to
establish whether the institution still offered
students a statement of purpose. Few did, beyond

paragraphs about the programs of the college to fit graduates for further study or gainful employment. When I asked faculty members of those colleges about their teaching, there was reference to values in most instances only in their observation that they were engaged in "value-free inquiry." By the 'seventies the authority of the university had grown so powerful that colleges were adopting its vocabulary, its emphasis on the major department as the student's spiritual home, and the measuring of a faculty member's worth by the list of his publications. I noticed that faculty members who had once been content to be called professor of history, professor of philosophy, professor of anthropology, professor of German, now preferred to be called historian, philosopher, anthropologist, Germanist. Such a choice of a title may, I suppose, be a reflection of our national preference for "doing" over "being," but I have believed that in our colleges the choice of such self-identification bespeaks a wish of the member to identify himself with the way of the university and the subordination of teaching to research.

It was, of course, the success of the German universities in fostering research that attracted Americans in the first place and which led to the development of American universities dominated by graduate schools and research activity. The shape of the modern university, particularly the public kind, is a pyramid, with a huge base of neglected undergraduates supporting the higher levels of graduate and professional schools, and at the very top the research professors who do no teaching whatsoever. The university's prestige is measured by the amount of funded research activity that is going on within its walls. Nobody, to the best of my knowledge, ever claims these days that a university is successful in educating its undergraduates; indeed the opposite is usually what is asserted. The current President of Harvard University was greeted at his installation in 2001 by a request from students that he do something, finally, about the poverty of undergraduate instruction in the University. From time to time somebody proposes that this or that university should take undergraduate education seriously, but the voice quickly dies away.

    One of my consultancies for NEH, with a department of history in a major university in the late 'seventies, began with the president's telling the three of us representing the Endowment that he was "totally committed" to the department's desire, set out in its appeal to the Endowment, to improve the quality of its teaching of undergraduates. The vice-president for academic affairs later voiced his support with similar emphasis, as did the dean. One or two of the full professors looked puzzled by the idea, but the majority was certainly ready to see the Endowment provide funds. Finally we came to the people who were actually doing the teaching, the untenured assistant professors, instructors, and graduate assistants; we were met with mocking laughter when we told them of the wish of the top brass to have them give greater attention to their teaching. The word had just come to them that one book would no longer be enough to get a person tenure. We recommended that the Endowment spend its funds elsewhere.

I do not wish to suggest by the foregoing or in any other way that research and teaching are not compatible when each is given appropriate weight. It is to state the obvious to say that every faculty member should have an ongoing research interest; the extended summer vacation is intended to provide time and opportunity for it, to say nothing of the sabbatical leave that is now standard virtually everywhere. The first question in any discussion of undergraduate, liberal education is how priorities shall be set. Nobody can doubt for a moment what the priority of the contemporary university is; it can be easily seen in its allocation of funds. The price that is paid for that priority was dramatically displayed in a photograph spread across the front page of the *Des Moines Register* a few years ago. The photographer had artfully placed himself behind an instructor who was addressing a freshman class, the picture showing a gigantic hall packed with row after row of students receding into an obscure distance. The caption beneath told the reader that there were more students in that hall than there were incorporated communities in the State of Iowa. The careful viewer could discern a few faces close to the front, some legs dangling over chair backs, a fellow cuddling a girl, some students evidently catching a nap. But the great number of students in the room were invisible. At what a remove is that contemporary reality from the nineteenth century claim that the best kind of education was the student on one end of a log and the President of Amherst College on the other. A couple of years after that photograph appeared, the same university was obliged, after countless complaints from students and their parents, to establish tests of standard spoken English for the teaching assistants it was inflicting on the undergraduates. The university was caught in a trap of needing to fund the overseas students who were being brought in to prop up the graduate school programs in several disciplines; having them teach the freshmen courses was its way.

    I was witness to a remarkable demonstration of the power of the university model. It was at a meeting in 1971 of the presidents of the consortium of liberal arts colleges to which Kenyon College belonged, which I attended as acting president. As soon as the meeting was called to order, one of our number, a man in his early thirties who was in his first semester in office, asked for the floor. To his quickly dumbfounded colleagues he presented this statement: "If we have any integrity, we shall immediately adjourn this meeting and return to our respective campuses, where we should at once begin to plan the dismantling of our institutions and the pooling of our resources in the interest of creating one half-decent university. I see no point in seeking to preserve what we are." He was an alumnus of the college he now led, a Wunderkind of sorts who had been admitted to graduate work in physics after only three undergraduate years. Obviously his college's practices had not persuaded him that there was more to education than mastering research techniques.

The answer of many a college these days, when asked what it is that distinguishes it from the university, is that the difference is no more than a matter of scale. Small classes, teaching done by experienced professors and not by graduate students, available lab space, open stacks in the library, professors the student can "get to know"—these are the advantages the small college can offer its students. But is that enough to justify the college's existence and what it must charge?

A First Question

There is really only one reason for the existence of the liberal arts college and that is to be an alternative to the university, but if all the college can say is that it teaches the same chemistry, English, history, anthropology that the university teaches, only less of it, it will not be persuasive. Even if it really can afford to offer the advantages that the small institution can bring, it will not be worthy of our society's support if it is merely doing the university's work on a small scale. But it seems clear that the preference of faculty members in many colleges these days is precisely to have the institution be a university on a small scale. More than one college has announced that it would cease billing itself as a liberal arts college and would henceforth be known as a "research college." We must assume that the choice of that label means a celebration of value-free inquiry and the pursuit of knowledge as an end in itself. It means, sad to say, that the college, abandoning liberal education, finds no purpose for itself other than to be a more comfortable and more intimate—perhaps even easier?—version of the university.

The power of the university way has grown remarkably since World War II and it has increasingly dominated discussion of higher education. It shapes most thinking about what should go on in higher education, argues what should be given priority, what shall be taught and how. Most damaging to the idea of liberal education, it insists that truth is within the single discipline. It has affected all institutions of learning in a greater or lesser degree and its power to control faculty thinking is the great opponent faced by a college which seeks to champion liberal education.

I have not, of course, wished, in describing the consequences for "the land of poets and thinkers" of the corruption of German education, to imply that the United States will inevitably have a Hitler. What I must argue, however, is that our universities and most of our colleges are failing to examine and champion the values liberal education so long proclaimed; they have thus contributed significantly to the dangerous egocentricity of our people and the amoral character of American society and its political life. "Where there is no vision," the Old Testament book warns, "the people perish." Higher education is not providing that vision of a free society which Jefferson believed was its prime task, nor is it producing leaders who will act out of a sense of their responsibility to their fellows. Nothing, Goethe said, can more alienate us from life than literature can; nothing can more firmly bind us to life than literature. So, I believe, it is with education. When we forget what Gordon Keith Chalmers of Kenyon College called "the particularly human terms" of the questions undergraduate education addresses, we risk that alienation and the cultivation of an amoral view of the world.

    I came to these conclusions only after many years in the academic profession. When I joined the faculty of Kenyon College in 1954 I knew as little of liberal education and the liberal arts college as I knew, still very much the immigrant, of Thomas Jefferson and the American idea of freedom. President Chalmers and the senior faculty who were my mentors, together with the authors who were my chief professional interest, brought me to shape the questions and to embrace the convictions which have been central to my life. Those same questions and convictions are central to the chapters that follow, and they ought now, I believe, to be central to discussions about undergraduate education everywhere, but particularly in our independent colleges.

Chapter II
Opposite Poles

In the late winter of 1954 I sat in the only chair of a small hotel room in New York City. A few feet away from me, on the edge of the only bed in the room, sat the President of Kenyon College, Gordon Keith Chalmers. He had insisted that I, a candidate for the German position in his small Department of Modern Languages, occupy the chair. He said he would be perfectly comfortable sitting on the bed. I was grateful to him.

For close to an hour Chalmers questioned me about what were for him the relevant elements of the biographical sketch I had submitted with my letter of application: my upbringing in a Yorkshire coal mining village; my seven years as a scholarship boy, commuting three miles on weekdays to Castleford Grammar School; my four years in the British army, two of them attached to American intelligence in Germany; my formal education subsequently at the University of Leeds in England, McGill University in Montreal, and finally Harvard. It didn't surprise me that, with memories of World War II and the concentration camps still fresh in everybody's mind, he was particularly interested in knowing why I had switched from French, my best subject in school, to German. The answer to his question, one I had been asked before, was the longest I made in that hour. My explanation seemed to satisfy him, and, after telling me of his own literary interests, he pressed on to ask me about my interest in Romanticism. We talked at some length about that great age in German culture, the time of Goethe, Beethoven, Kant, and other giants. He acknowledged that his German wasn't good enough for him to be able to penetrate Goethe's *Faust* and I acknowledged in turn that my own efforts to come to terms with that monster of a work still continued. His smiles and occasional nods of the head were reassuring.

Traveling back on the train to Massachusetts, I found myself thinking I had really learned nothing about Kenyon College in our session to add to what I had culled from a catalogue I had found at Harvard. But I was greatly impressed that its President spent his time interviewing candidates for faculty positions. (I walked past the official residence of Harvard's President nearly every day, but I had never set eyes on him.) I was no less impressed by the breadth of Chalmers's interests and understanding. Whether I was invited out to Kenyon for more interviewing or not, I had certainly enjoyed the interview and I was proud of myself for having got through it without desperately needing a cigarette.

But, oh, how I wanted to be invited out to Gambier, Ohio. I needed to get away from

Harvard. When I was offered a four-year fellowship there, as I was finishing my master's degree at McGill, I thought I knew enough about Harvard to believe that it was where I would wish to be forever. Thirty months later I had lost all affection for the place and was nearly desperate to get a job elsewhere. And this at a time, sad to say, when positions in German were as scarce as hen's teeth. Indeed, one of the first things I had been told when I came down from Canada was that there were no jobs in German. Period. America's faculties, rapidly expanded after 1945 as returning veterans flowed onto the campuses, had been as quickly shrunken when the last veterans graduated.

In my student years in England and Canada I had been generously educated in three literatures, particularly by my major professor at McGill, who always insisted that ideas didn't stop at the Rhine or the English Channel and that a literary work was best placed in the largest context of understanding we could provide for it. He saw to it that I didn't settle comfortably into the single study of German literature. On the reading lists for those majoring in German appeared the great Russians, together with Ibsen, Zola, Rousseau, and others whose writings could help illuminate the German works that were our prime study. He put me into year-long courses in philosophy, on Shakespeare, and Greek and

Roman literature in translation. He invited me to follow the Romantics into the epic poetry of the Middle Ages and to heed their assertion that the German soul could best be reached through German music.

With him, Willem Graff, I served an apprenticeship to German culture and its larger European context, even more when I became a candidate for the master's degree. It suited his temperament and mine that I should write my master's thesis on Goethe and Shakespeare.

Graff was a Hollander who had grown up in a village on the German border, speaking both languages with equal fluency from childhood. He had earned a doctorate at a German university before leaving Europe for Canada in the 'thirties. McGill was a much smaller institution in my years there than it is today, with but one doctoral program and few candidates for M.A. degrees; it was more like the English universities of those days than the American, with a prime emphasis on undergraduates. Graff's was a small department—he had only two colleagues in German—but his department didn't define the limits of his activity. I sat in on a guest lecture on Nietzsche he gave to the majors and graduate students in philosophy—the only time I heard him lecture in English—and I know that he often appeared before history classes. He taught out of a love for language and literature that was inspiring. I can say confidently that he shaped me more than any other teacher did, opening ever larger worlds to me. I expected more of the same in Harvard's much bigger and more celebrated community of scholars.

I was quickly disillusioned. At Harvard I felt myself shrunken, the captive of a department that set tight boundaries about itself, in an institution where departments seemed to coexist without ever touching on one another. At the end of my first semester the chairman of the Department called me to his office. He wished me to know that he and his colleagues were distressed by my practice of alluding, in papers and oral presentations in seminars, to English and French authors. They would prefer that I limit my references to German writers and thinkers. I was so taken aback that I didn't try to defend myself against the implicit charge that I had been trying to show off. I found such parallels genuinely interesting and, more importantly, enlightening. But by this time I knew on which side my professional bread was buttered; I ought to have heeded more carefully the warnings I had been given by my fellow graduate students about the Department's isolating behaviors.

It was they, my fellow sufferers, who made my three years at Harvard tolerable and who helped to convince me not to abandon the place at the end of my second year, when I was invited to take a job at a university in Nova Scotia. Though I was finished with my seminar work by then and ready to begin the research for my dissertation, I recognized that, were I to succumb to the temptation and leave, I might suffer the fate of those grey figures I occasionally saw visiting the Department. They were candidates for the degree who, after as many as a dozen years, were still not finished, their dissertations pushed aside by the demands of job, marriage, child rearing. The Department did not love such people, preferring those who left after four years with degree in hand or at least with the work on their dissertation nearly completed.

There were few resident candidates for the doctorate in German literature and thought. In my entering year there were only five of us; there were three or four a year or two ahead of us. Falling by the wayside was commonplace among graduate students of any kind, but particularly in the humanities, and some of my fellows dropped out before the end of the second year. Only two of us persisted to the final goal of the degree.

We graduate students in German were a mixed lot of immigrants and natives, the American citizens in the majority by a slim margin. By a slight margin again men were in the majority. Apart from the fact that we were Germanophiles, which is why we were there in the first place, there were two bonds that joined us together. The first was a sense of being in servitude to a system we loathed, working for what was derisively called "the union card." We all knew that we needed the degree which would open the door to a job and the hope for tenure. We all lived with the anxious knowledge that the Department's professors had the power of life and death over us and that we must above all else please them in everything we did. Though all of us chafed at seminars on minor poets or at the number of required courses on the history of the German language, which seemed to have little relevance to our literary interests and pursuits, we curried the favor of the senior faculty members. Never far from our minds was the knowledge that we should have to face these men on our pre-thesis orals and again at the defense of our thesis. We exchanged helpful bits of information about their idiosyncrasies and prejudices. Above all we knew that we must at all times fly the Department flag, speak German whenever we were in hearing distance of a certain professor, and never be seen in the company of a member of another department. I came slowly to recognize that the senior members thought of the Department—and wished us to see ourselves—as an extension of the

German university system, having only tangentially to do with higher education in America.

The second bond, for most of us, was our teaching. Like some of my fellows, I was being supported largely by a working wife, who had been my sole support after my English equivalent of the GI Bill ran out at the end of my undergraduate years. We "teaching fellows" were paid $400 a year per course, which meant that we had to teach two courses just to pay our tuition. (That Harvard didn't simply waive our tuition meant that our earnings were taxable, another reason for our feeling that the University didn't care a fig about us.) In my second and third years I taught four sections, two of introductory German, two intermediate, which was the equal of an instructor's full load—for which he was paid $4,000, while I earned $1,600. The teaching I did was a very valuable part of my Harvard experience, much of that coming from my comparing notes with my colleagues who were also cutting teeth on Harvard's undergraduates. I came early to wonder why it was that so much of the teaching of those carefully selected students was in the hands of neophytes. I was constantly frustrated, though, by the fact that we were shifted from one section to another at the end of the first semester. By the time I was getting to know my students, they disappeared into the Harvard Yard, never to be seen again.

It was some years later that a professor at the University of Chicago was heard to declare that the mere sight of an undergraduate made him want to throw up, but that might have been said by any one of the professors of German, who kept themselves aloof from the undergraduate program of the Department. And aloof from the graduate students as well, for the most part. The strongest memory I have of my thesis adviser, whose written comments on drafts of my dissertation were invariably helpful, was of his retreating from me foot by foot whenever I attempted to catch him for a brief question after a seminar session. We forgave this sort of behavior in some measure though, because we knew that "publish or perish" meant nearly as much for the Department's senior members as it did for the juniors. Teaching could not possibly be a priority for anybody who was seeking to make a career at Harvard.

With those juniors, an untenured trio of two instructors and an assistant professor, we had a comfortable relationship. We shared with them, in lieu of office space, a small room in Sever Hall where there was a conference table and chairs, as well as a set of pigeon-holes where our official mail was delivered. (The tenured members, on the other hand, not only had private offices in the Busch-Reisinger Museum, the home of the

Department, but also second offices in Widener Library, where they would not be interrupted by students or colleagues as they did their serious work.) We felt a sympathetic bond with the juniors, for their future was as uncertain as our own. Many were called to Harvard, but few were chosen. It was apparent to everybody that no more than one of the three juniors would advance, if that. We grieved in particular for the assistant professor, one of the brightest men I have ever known, for he had somehow crossed the most feared of the senior members, earning his displeasure. With that his fate was sealed. No matter what recognition his publications might earn him, there would be no Harvard in his future. Indeed, it was whispered about that his nemesis would see to it that no Ivy League university would hire him either.

Paranoia? Perhaps. But our workaday conversations and the social evenings we spent together occasionally on weekends were filled with such imaginings. As one of our number completed course requirements and was ready to take pre-thesis orals, our anxious talk about him centered not on whether his command of the material would be enough to satisfy, but on what piece of trivia might be thrown at him to put him off balance and make him flounder. When my own turn came, I was doing pretty well until

I was asked whether I knew why a minor seventeenth-century German poet died in Vienna. I didn't, I had to admit. Because he had gone there to consult a certain physician, as any serious scholar would know. Ah, literature!

That was the kind of thing that kept me constantly furious at the Department. There seemed to be a conspiracy to reduce us. It was as though the love for the German language and literature that we had all brought with us was being deliberately squeezed out of us by the demand that we focus on biographical data, on scholarly disagreements, on minor authors. How often did we lament to one another that the greats of German literature were not discussed in any formal setting. We knew the reason, of course: seminar topics had more to do with whatever research a professor was doing than with the needs of us students. Besides, we were not there for the central, the essential, but to prepare ourselves, in a favorite phrase of a senior professor, "to contribute our little brick to the edifice of German scholarship."

So we fell back on one another. It is often claimed that students at every level learn a great deal from one another and I certainly learned more that I valued from my fellows—bright, intelligent, informed graduates of some of the country's best colleges and universities—than I did from my professors. To one of them, a kind New Englander and ardent lover of things German, I am particularly indebted, for he introduced me to an American idea that has been central to my professional life. He listened sympathetically one day as I declared, in the depths of my despair, that I could not find any joy in thinking of a career in which I would be narrowed by the department that employed me, so that my teaching would be limited to those Romantic poets I had made my specialty. I wanted to teach them, yes, but I also wanted to teach the lyrics of Walther von der Vogelweide, that genius of medieval poetry; to teach Goethe and Thomas Mann; in short, to range over the greatest literature Germans had produced, even though I knew that only attention to my "little brick" could earn me tenure in some university. My friend had a quick response. "You don't belong in a university," he said. "You should be in a liberal arts college."

I was puzzled. "Liberal arts college" meant nothing to me; it was not part of the vocabulary I had brought from England. In England and Canada we talked of the "arts and sciences"; "liberal" for me was a word from politics. In my little Yorkshire world "college" had but one meaning: a teachers' training college, a two-year institution which prepared people to be schoolteachers and granted a diploma rather than a degree. (I had yet to learn that "school," "college," and "university" were virtually interchangeable terms in this country, and that people could appropriate them at will for even bizarre activities.) My friend explained the purely undergraduate nature of the liberal arts college, an institution concerned to have its students pursue their special interest in a broad cultural framework. He spoke enthusiastically of the years he had spent in such a college before World War II and of professors who were more McGill than Harvard. Invariably small and often church-related, these colleges were to be found in the dozens all over New England and on into the Midwest. I was intrigued. Perhaps I wouldn't have to give up on academe after all and go to work for the CIA, a notion that had pushed itself more and more into my thinking about a future. But prudence argued that, before I made any serious inquiry into a career in a liberal arts college, I had better get more work done on my dissertation.

 Crucial for any graduate student in the humanities is finding a manageable thesis topic, to say nothing of identifying a faculty member who will win the department's approval for the topic and offer benevolent supervision. I was immensely fortunate in both respects. Virtually all the graduate students who were on the literature track, rather than the philological, had opted to write under the spreading wings of Heinrich Schneider, an internationally recognized authority on G.E. Lessing, the Enlightenment thinker whose play, *Nathan der Weise*, was the first German work to portray a Jew sympathetically. He seemed to have an endless number of topics that could be developed into dissertations and, besides, he was known to have an extraordinarily large number of contacts among fellow refugees from Nazi Germany who had found homes in America's universities. Much was to be said, then, for asking Schneider for a topic, but he fitted neither my interest in the Romantics nor my idea of a sympathetic supervisor. (He was to give me a bad few minutes before I left Harvard, when he told me I was a unicum, and then demanded that I tell him why he labeled me that. When I foundered, he told me that I was the only graduate student in his fifteen years at Harvard to get a job without a letter of recommendation from him.)

I turned instead to Stuart Atkins, the Department's authority on Romanticism who had recently become its chairman. I was the first doctoral candidate to work with him. My fellow students found his sometimes frosty smile and his austere manner off-putting. But I had been attracted from the first by his insistence, with the New Critics, on the value of close and careful reading of literary texts.

With Atkins's blessing I made good headway in my third year, sufficient to allow me to think seriously about and have an eye open for an opportunity in a liberal arts college that would allow me to leave Harvard early. My mentioning this to one of the instructors, who had already begun putting out feelers, led him to alert me to the Kenyon opening. He was not interested in it himself, for Kenyon lay in that hinterland into which no self-respecting would-be Ivy Leaguer would venture. It was the only opening in a liberal arts college that I had heard of that year.

The invitation to Gambier I had so ardently wished for came a few days after my New York interview in the form of a phone call from the President's secretary. I was asked to be at Kenyon late in the day the following Saturday, with interviews on Sunday morning and early afternoon, and a departure time that would allow me to get back in time to teach my Monday classes. The secretary offered to make my travel arrangements, but, perhaps wishing to demonstrate what a self-starter of a candidate I was, I declined her offer. I should have taken it. I found myself eventually determining that to get to Gambier, Ohio, was no easy thing: a plane from Boston to New York, another to Columbus, a fifty-mile bus ride to Mount Vernon, and a taxi for the last six miles to Gambier.

Kenyon College celebrates its founder in a happy song that begins, "The first of Kenyon's goodly race/Was that great man, Philander Chase," and great he was, both in physical stature—a six-six, three-hundred pounder—and vision. Wishing to prepare young men to bring God's word to the heathen Indian and imbued with Rousseaunian suspicion of a corrupting society, he thought it crucial to remove his students from the temptations of the city. So he searched for, and in 1826 he found, a hilltop in the wilderness. He planned to create there a virtually self-contained academic community where teachers and students alike would cut down trees, cultivate crops, and take care of livestock. With the blessing of the Episcopal Church, Bishop Chase sailed off to England to raise money to build the College; reminders of his success as a fund raiser exist in English names like Kenyon, Rosse, Bexley, as well as in the name of the village that is merely an extension of the College. There is a whiff of England about Kenyon to this day.

I reflected on this history as I was carried towards Columbus. I wondered how Kenyon was able to attract 1954's young men—the College had remained all-male—to such a remote place. I was still the captive of European standards of distance and travel times between places, which my years in Massachusetts had not altered. I was also used to universities that were surrounded by the bustle of cities, rubbing elbows with the workaday world. That world seemed far away from Gambier, Ohio, but then the world often seemed at a far remove from the Harvard Yard, and even farther from the German Department.

My interviews next morning, the first with three of the members of the small department I was hoping to join, were comfortable and pleasant. I was gently quizzed about the state of my dissertation, my interests, and my history, but I was urged to ask questions and I did. I was struck by how little reference there was to the department and how, instead, it was the College that these men regarded as the locus of their activity. "Colleagues" was a word the three of them used frequently and it was quickly apparent that they meant professors all across the departments, not just the people at that table. But I was even more struck by how often they spoke of President Chalmers, remarking among other things on his requiring every student, even those from the immediate vicinity, to be in residence.

I learned, too, that all members of the faculty and staff were required to be in residence, in houses or apartments supplied by the College, this in lieu of part salary. The practice was a survival of the Bishop's idea of a community focused upon its work. On a walk about the village, James Browne, the department chair, pointed out white barracks, given to Kenyon by the government after the war, when Kenyon's enrollment soared to six hundred and there was urgent need of housing. Now they were occupied by seminary students and some junior faculty members. For most entering faculty members a couple of years in the barracks was part of initiation. Some of the faculty residences Browne had pointed out seemed pretty grand and, after some of the quarters my wife and I had occupied in our six years of impoverished married life, even the barracks didn't look so bad.

Our walk had begun at Old Kenyon, the first building Philander Chase had erected. It had suffered a disastrous fire in 1949 and was afterwards restored stone by stone and given a modern interior. Nine students had died in the fire; to understand the impact upon the community, that figure has to be put in the context of a student body that numbered under six hundred. The College, I was to learn, had never recovered financially from the disaster and any mention of the fire revived sorrow.

The place was small, no doubt about it. And clearly it had its limits. Lunching with the bachelors of the faculty in the Great Hall (a reproduction of an Oxford refectory, I was quickly told), I was asked by a junior member of the Philosophy Department, an immigrant from France and recent Harvard Ph.D., "Are you marry-ed?" When I said that I was, he nodded approvingly, adding that Gambier was no place to be not marry-ed. His two colleagues, much older and apparently content in their bachelordom, offered no comment. There was obviously nothing to Gambier other than Kenyon College. All that the village had to offer by way of commerce was contained within two blocks on the main street: a gas station, two grocery stores, a bank, a restaurant, the post office, and a used book shop where a handsome sign advertised "Denham Sutcliffe, Bookseller." My mind recorded a very familiar Yorkshire surname.

Yet, for all its limits, Gambier, with its faded New England charm, was an easy place to fall in love with and fall I did. The College's handsome stone buildings, ivy covered, were spaced at large intervals about the College Park—never called the campus, Browne emphasized—and there were trees, tall and spreading, everywhere. There was a sense of permanence, of tradition, of solidity. Earlier mention of the seminary had prepared me to see the Church of the Holy Spirit across from the President's residence, but it prompted me, as we walked by, to ask Browne about the influence of the Episcopal Church on the life of the

College. He was quick to say that there was none, even though the Bishop of Ohio and the Bishop of Southern Ohio served in alternate years as chairman of the board of trustees. Nobody, he went on, counted faculty heads in church on a Sunday morning; few members of the faculty belonged to the congregation. Students, though, were required to attend Sunday morning services for half the number of Sundays in the semester, which seemed to my still English mind a curious expectation for an academic institution to have of its students. But it joined with what I had learned at breakfast was a requirement that students have a year of physical education and demonstrate that they could swim a length of the pool. It had never occurred to me to ask whether Harvard undergraduates faced similar requirements, but then Harvard students existed for me only to the extent that they were in the classes I taught.

The Catalogue had told me that Frank Bailey, Dean of the College, was a Dartmouth graduate and a Harvard Ph.D. in history. We met him as he got out of his station wagon at Ascension Hall, where classes were taught in the humanities and social sciences and where the faculties of those divisions had their offices. Ascension—the Episcopal Church in evidence again—housed most of the working part of the College except the lab sciences, which were in a handsome building on the other side of Middle Path; that gravel-clad walk ran through the Park and the village in a straight line to Bexley Hall, home of the seminary.

Dean Bailey walked with a marked limp; he had a back problem from his navy days in WWII which had been worsened by his heroic efforts to rescue students from Old Kenyon's flames. He was an immediately likeable man, peppery New England, a gruff exterior but gentle in his questioning. We smoked our way through an hour of easy conversation, an interview as unlike the one I had had with Chalmers as it was possible to imagine. Bailey spent nearly all the time asking me about my personal life and preferences—and about my wife. It was an interview such as no dean would dare conduct today. He was interested in the me outside my discipline: did I enjoy sports, what kinds of books did I read for pleasure, what were my wife's interests, did we plan to have children, where did our families live, did I plan on becoming an American citizen, what would I wish to be doing ten years from now. He confessed that he liked to have family men on the faculty, men who would want to make careers at Kenyon. He did, to be sure, talk about what would be expected of the appointee: the number and type of courses to be taught in the year, the responsibilities of faculty members to advise freshmen and sophomores outside their departments, to be part of the life of the community. His approving nods when I answered and his easy manner with me gave me hope that I was going to get his vote, though I wondered later whether, in the Kenyon scheme of things, anybody's vote besides the President's would carry great weight.

President Chalmers, it was quickly clear when Browne delivered me to his home in mid-afternoon, knew all about me he wished to know. There was to be no more interviewing. He was most cordial, wishing to know how I had enjoyed my visit and enquiring about my departure. When I spoke of the arrangements for my return journey he looked pained. "We can't have that," he said and went on to say that the overnight train to Boston was a far better way to travel. He sped off and came back a few minutes later, having made arrangements for a College car to take me to the railroad station. His final words to me were, "We are very much interested in your candidacy," a line I stole and used again and again in later years, when, as Kenyon's Dean and Provost, I said farewell to candidates I hoped to bring to the faculty.

Chalmers was right about the superiority of going back by train, but I didn't sleep much as we chugged the five hundred miles. My head was spinning with thoughts of my visit. Kenyon had captured me and I wanted the job there more than

I had ever imagined I would wish to have a particular position. The opportunity to develop a program in German literature was exciting enough. I had ambivalent feelings about being the one and only in German, but I was already imagining the possibility of a colleague as the program developed. I had been most happily impressed by the sense of collegiality there; it was what I had imagined when I had first thought of an academic career. And there was the charm of the place and its physical beauty. I was certain that Chalmers and Bailey were men I could work with. I was no less certain that Gordon Keith Chalmers would be the one who would decide my fate. But I had decided I very much wanted to work for his Kenyon.

When the envelope came from his office a few days later I could tell by its weight that it had to be good news. Seeing its contents gave me one of the happiest moments of my life. I was to become Assistant Professor of Modern Languages, on an initial two-year appointment in a tenure track position, with a most generous starting salary of $4,500 and housing provided by the College. (At that time Harvard was employing beginning instructors, with Ph.D. already in hand, at a salary of $4,000 and no housing.) Kenyon obviously wanted me. It would have me, body and soul, for twenty-six years.

Chapter III
Visionary Leadership

If ever an institution was properly called "the lengthened shadow of one man," it was Kenyon College in the nineteen years that Gordon Chalmers was its president. Even his critics recognized that he was in every respect a very remarkable leader.

He had been elected a Rhodes Scholar in 1925 and had spent three years at Oxford when that ancient and rightly honored university had fallen under the spell of an idealistic liberalism that fostered, side by side, a faith in pacifism, an uncritical admiration of Stalin and the Soviet Union, and the belief that fascism was the wave of the future. Chalmers never forgot or forgave such thinkers, in Britain or in this country, those who between the two world wars abandoned faith in liberty and surrendered themselves to belief in the coming triumph of dictatorial regimes. The fatal flaw in their thinking, he would later argue, came from their having embraced a neo-Rousseaunian belief that man was not responsible for the evil in the world, for man was by nature good; the evil was due entirely to the social organizations under which he had been forced to live. Attacking that dogma and championing a form of education that would focus on understanding human nature in its fullness and the individual's capacity for both good and evil became his life's work.

I remember when the instructions to those who were preparing letters of support for candidates for the Rhodes told us that the examiners were not looking for pale "laureates of the classroom." I have always cherished the phrase. The examiners wanted more than the promising scholar. They preferred candidates who were, besides, comfortable in the world beyond the academy, who were fond of "manly sports," and who would use their advantaged position to look out on the world and imagine how they might seek to change it for the better.

The young Chalmers must have delighted the examiners. When I knew him, in his early fifties, he still radiated energy and purpose. He was a stockily built man with a strong physique, a disciplined body. He always walked zestfully along Middle Path on his way to his office in Ascension Hall. Seeing him bounce along, I thought that he looked like a still-active soccer player, for he seemed to be thrusting himself towards a goal. The same energy was always evident in his speeches and his writing, both the products of rigorous thinking. I have found it difficult to think of a Chalmers relaxed, a Chalmers making small talk, a Chalmers who was anything but the dynamo of Kenyon College. For I never knew him socially; I saw him only at a distance, in monthly faculty meetings, on platforms and by podiums, at the official occasions of the College. Time might have afforded me the knowledge of him that trusted confidants among the senior faculty enjoyed, but only twenty months after I became a member of the College—his term for faculty and students alike—Gordon Chalmers was suddenly and unexpectedly gone, falling dead in the street on a May afternoon in 1956 in Hyannis, Massachusetts. He was only fifty-two years old.

On that evening, as word of the President's death spread about Gambier, the shared telephone "party lines" were tied up for hours. Faculty members—and their wives—asked one another anxiously what would become of Kenyon now, whether it could survive without him. My own joy in having just defended my dissertation at Harvard, without pain or embarrassment, was swept away by my colleagues' grief and anxiety. After the brief security that had come with knowing that I was now *Herr Doktor Professor*, I felt the ground beneath my feet becoming shaky. Only in the anxious days that followed did it become fully clear to me how completely the College I had so happily embraced was the Kenyon of President Chalmers.

He seemed to have come to Gambier in 1937 with the clear intention of transforming

Kenyon. It was then a comfortable, though quite respectable, college for the sons of well-to-do Episcopalians, perhaps best known for having a school of aeronautics (some students owned planes) and a polo team (some students owned horses). Its name was not mentioned in the company of Amherst, Haverford, Williams. Chalmers quickly set about turning it into the liberal arts college his mind had already shaped out of his reactions to his Oxford years and the shortcomings of the American educational system he readily identified.

In choosing Chalmers, only thirty-three years old but with a three-year term as President of Rockford College nearly completed, the trustees had broken with a long tradition. Ending the line of Episcopal priests in the office, they opted clearly and certainly for an ambitious leader with impeccable academic credentials: B.A. Brown, M.A. Oxford, Ph.D. Harvard, a proven teacher at Mount Holyoke College. But that did not say that they, like so many trustees at other colleges before and since, were breaking the ties that for over a century had bonded College and Church; nor did Chalmers seek that. He was a convinced Christian who was comfortable being head of the seminary as well as of the undergraduate division. It is telling that he always required the College chaplain to report directly to him. He preached sermons from time to time in the Church of the Holy Spirit. In that same building he held the official Opening of College each fall and the baccalaureate service in June; they were alike occasions for him to address the students and his colleagues of the faculty on the College's mission. But he never muddied the waters by having assemblies in the Church or by requiring that members of the College be believers. The only faith he asked faculty members to share with him was his burning faith in liberal education.

Chalmers lost no time in seeking to build a name for Kenyon as a place where work of the first order would be undertaken. Within a year of his inauguration he had persuaded John Crowe Ransom to leave Vanderbilt University and to come to Kenyon as Professor of Poetry. (Chalmers preferred to use "poetry" for all imaginative literature.) It is easy to think that nothing Chalmers did thereafter was as important to the building of Kenyon's reputation as luring Ransom to Gambier. Within a year the plan for the literary magazine that the world was to know as *The Kenyon Review* was developed. It was to be the emblem of the President's conviction that the study of "poetry" was central to the College's work. The journal began publication in 1939 and was soon recognized as preeminent among its kind. In its pages appeared the living giants of American literature: Robert Lowell (who had left Harvard to study with Ransom at Kenyon), Robert Penn Warren, Richard Ellmann, Randall Jarrell, and many others. Soon prominent European writers made their appearance in the magazine's pages; its subscription list after WWII spread around the globe. Importantly, the *Review* was to become the premier vehicle for the New Criticism as well as for the work of emerging writers; its influence on American letters in the 'forties and 'fifties was immeasurable.

Robert Frost, Chalmers's fellow New Englander and close friend for many years, helped to burnish Kenyon's reputation. He was a frequent visitor to the College and writer-in-residence for a term in the spring of 1941. There were many other prominent visitors to Gambier during Chalmers's tenure, some of them brought there by the Conference on the Heritage of the English-Speaking Peoples he organized in 1946, even more of them coming to the Summer School of English, which ran for three summers between 1948 and 1950. I have been impressed over the years by the number of people I have met, in and out of academe, who have remembered appreciatively the hours they spent at Kenyon in the company of the nation's best known poets and critics.

Nineteen thirty-eight was a banner year for new appointments to the Kenyon faculty, as

Chalmers exploited the American Oxonian network to put him in touch with the kind of men he wanted as colleagues. Prominent among them was Philip Blair Rice, an Oxford man brought in as professor of philosophy and managing editor of the *Review*, after years of working as a newspaperman in Cincinnati. That same year brought Charles Thornton to the Biology Department, where he was to inspire several generations of future scientists; Rhodes Scholar Bayes Norton, a professor of chemistry who was to become a major figure in the development of the Advanced Placement Program; Randall Jarrell, already a recognized poet, in English; and a refugee from Nazi Germany, Richard Salomon, who held joint appointments in history and church history at the College and at the seminary, and who was to seem to Kenyon students in later years a giant of scholarship. I was to know nearly all these men well and I came to know their allegiance to the President's idea of what was to be expected of the faculty member in the liberal arts college.

It was with the appointment of like-minded faculty members that Chalmers began, with the plan, as Kenyon's reputation rose, to increase the student body from three hundred to what he thought of as an "ideal" five hundred. But all of his plans were shattered by Pearl Harbor. For a time it seemed certain that the war would destroy Kenyon (as the American Civil War destroyed Philander Chase's second creation, Jubilee College in Illinois). But the United States Army proved willing to work with Chalmers to develop a program which would keep the large number of faculty at the College in teaching roles and permit a limited course offering for students to go forward to the degree, even while the major activity in Gambier became the training of future officers in a meteorology program.

Chalmers remained in office, seeking to hold together a cadre of people on which a post-war Kenyon could be rebuilt. For a few years after 1945 students poured in, most of them veterans supported by the GI Bill. Enrollment topped six hundred, straining every facility. New faculty members were recruited, prominent among them another Rhodes Scholar, Denham Sutcliffe, who was serving as director of freshman English at Harvard when Chalmers persuaded him that he would flourish in Gambier. He was to become the one who, after Chalmers died, spoke more than any other to keeping the Chalmers Kenyon alive.

In those often hectic post-war years Chalmers was busy speaking and writing on the problems he saw in both secondary and higher education. He was a moving force in his professional organizations and known to a thoughtful public beyond academe. Denham Sutcliffe, who occasionally accompanied Chalmers to meetings of college and university presidents, told me years later that Chalmers "cut as broad a swath as the President of Harvard."

In those same years Chalmers became more and more concerned that the brightest and best among America's youth were being denied the education that was their birthright. In particular he fretted that the failures of the secondary schools, dominated by the Deweyites he abhorred, were obliging the colleges and universities to spend ever more time on remedial work, teaching the sort of English and math courses that were properly the business of the secondary school. His concerns were shared by his good friend President Hutchins of the University of Chicago, a frequent guest in Gambier during WWII. But the two reformers, who were preaching the same gospel to their undergraduate faculty, divided on how to deal with the problem of the gifted student cooling his heels in secondary school. Hutchins chose to admit youngsters of thirteen or fourteen directly to his institution's standard fare.

Chalmers, fearing for the social development of very young people plunged into the life of a college dormitory, argued instead that schools and colleges alike would profit if special courses could be offered in secondary schools, challenging the best students. His thinking eventually translated into what is called today the Advanced Placement Program, but was first known as the Kenyon Plan. Chalmers persuaded the presidents of a dozen distinguished colleges and the headmasters of a small number of secondary schools to join him in an experiment: to demonstrate that gifted high school seniors could successfully do the work ordinarily associated with the freshman courses in the best colleges and universities. As college freshmen then they would be credited with having done the work of introductory courses and thus be able to follow a richer course of study in their four years. Let me emphasize that: *a richer course of study in their four undergraduate years.* The program, administered by Educational Testing Service, was quickly a success, first in the east where nearly all the pioneering colleges and schools were located. But Chalmers's purpose was nearly as quickly ignored by some colleges and universities that came later to the program. Some faculty members saw it as an opportunity for their best pupils to move through the undergraduate curriculum in three years and get on to graduate school. Some administrators seized on acceleration as a selling point to prospective students and their parents. As going on beyond the bachelor's degree was seen more and more as a necessity, the idea of "accelerating" became increasingly popular. There are few places today where Chalmers's idea of greater enrichment and depth of experience is honored.

Whatever the merits or failings of the Advanced Placement Program, with which several of us at Kenyon remained involved for many years, it certainly helped to bring attention to the College and to enhance Gordon Chalmers's reputation as a visionary leader. Kenyon was finally seen as one of the country's foremost colleges and Chalmers a leader in the movement to bring higher standards to education at every level. In 1956 the *Chicago Tribune,* after concluding a national survey, called Kenyon the third best men's college in the nation, ranking it after only Haverford and Amherst. It is sadly ironic that this recognition, surely a triumph for Chalmers, came in the year of his death.

Four years earlier Chalmers had published his only book, *The Republic and the Person.* Its subtitle proposes that it is a discussion of the "necessities in modern American education." We can call it simply and accurately his philosophy of education, an implicit blueprint for the essential college. While many sections of the book, to be sure, are written specifically in response to particular aspects of certain reports and studies, most prominently the Report of the President's Commission on Higher Education published in 1947/48, it is in the first instance a sustained argument for the liberal arts college. He quickly defines his purpose as proposing a form of education for "responsible American liberalism" in specific contrast to the "disjointed liberalism" he had found at Oxford and which, to his dismay, had a strong grip on the schools and colleges of this country. For Chalmers liberal education meant a purposeful form of education: to ensure that Americans would understand, and be willing to fight to protect, the idea of liberty which is the foundation of the Republic. He puts this directly on an early page: "To understand that the 'self-evident truths' will be understood as well as reiterated dogmatically is the necessary national task of education." That is one of the timeless propositions in a work that was written when the Cold War and national responses to the threat of the Soviet Union were our daily headlines. His fear was that American educators had not only neglected, but had actually forgotten, that central responsibility.

 Like Thomas Jefferson, Chalmers believed the liberal arts college to be a crucial institution of American life, for the Republic could be protected only by leaders educated to understand the nation's identity. But that could come only when students had been brought to understand the nature of mankind. How else could they argue for the superiority of our republican form of government, the rightness of our Constitution? Instead of schools and colleges addressing themselves to that task, he found them seeking to shape the thinking of their students so as to have them embrace populist social theories: "The general object of education has become more and more to condition the mass attitudes toward specific social improvements, and enthusiasm for those reforms has diverted energy from the ancient and central task of converting the reason—of converting it from the knowledge and love of what is mean [vulgar] to the knowledge and love of what is worthy."

Such sentiments would doubtless today have Chalmers branded an elitist, a reactionary, a man with his head in the sand. He was none of these. He considered himself a liberal, and a classic liberal he was, in his constant championing of the freedoms afforded under the Constitution. Liberal he was too in asserting that the kind of education he spoke for was not one accessible only to the children of a ruling class; his years in England had made him an enemy of the class system and its limiting higher education to the aristocracy of birth or of wealth. The average American youth, he was convinced, was quite capable of dealing with the central questions in liberal education and, indeed, should be *required* to deal with them. He defines succinctly the purpose of the liberal society: "The liberal aim is, of course, to increase the number of individuals who are competent to think and act on their own. To many in education this aim means only skill in thinking. But it involves as well the ability to establish for one's self a standard by which to determine what is most worth thinking about and doing."

The title Chalmers chose for his book points to the essential identity of free person and Republic, the interdependence of two crucial ideas. His continuing, basic assertion is that the Republic will surely fail unless the individual is free and that assertion is central to all thinking about the nation; there will, simultaneously, be no free person unless the Republic exists to guarantee life and liberty. "The proper study of Americans is liberty … our central aim ought [therefore] to be the understanding of man, his nature, and place." Chalmers never confused liberty and license. For him, the idea of liberty always embraced responsibility to others. The individual must be free to act, but always willing to accept responsibility for that action, always willing to defend it by demonstrating that it had been taken only after rigorous reflection on its possible consequences. Ever mindful of the subjugation of those who had lived and still lived under dictatorial governments, Chalmers feared that our system of education was seeking to condition students to accept unthinkingly the mass movements of the age. He saw schools and colleges teaching "adjustment" to those movements. They should and must have a different aim: "Our greatest schools had been founded precisely in order that the young would not be content to adjust themselves to society, but would set about with vigor and courage to adjust society when they saw it in need of change."

The President's Commission of 1947-48 anticipated tendencies in education of the 'sixties and 'seventies when it stated: "The student and his rounded development will be at the center of institutional activities and subject matter at the periphery." Chalmers found the notion abhorrent and set against it his own institution's aim: "At Kenyon College we hold the reverse to be true: that a young man makes a step in his development if for the time being he forgets himself in beginning to master a few of the central disciplines of the mind." In comparable passages throughout his book Chalmers reiterates his conviction that the best service a college can provide its students is having them rigorously confront the demands of dealing with great, fundamental questions. He makes abundantly clear, too, that such engagement is not only, as so many college catalogues have proclaimed over the decades, to improve the student's ability to think independently. It is to have the student understand that the greater purpose of education is moral action.

That idea, novel to me when I first heard Chalmers argue it, has commanded my thinking about higher education ever since. It has not been a widely held view and is far less so today than it was in Chalmers's lifetime. But in many an address to campus audiences and service clubs I have elaborated on the argument Chalmers set forth clearly in 1952: "It is altogether possible that despite the fanfare of postwar reform the American educational system will continue to promote moral adolescence. That is the first danger of the present, the danger most pertinent to society and politics and most appropriate to be dealt with by education. For the proper object of school and college is moral maturity."

The reader will not find in *The Republic and the Person* a sketch of the ideal curriculum for the liberal arts college; there is no description in terms of so many courses in X and Y, this and that in the freshman year, that and the other in the sophomore year. For Chalmers liberal education was not something to be subdivided, not something contained within a particular course sequence. He thought of a process that continued formally throughout the full four years and, in private reading and engagement with ideas, for a lifetime. As much as what was studied was how it was studied, and why. "To pursue the study requires some decision about what subjects are of first importance, some specification of the ends to be sought within each subject, and some particulars of the manner in which the studies should be pursued." There were certain indispensable studies. He was strongly convinced that the humanities were central to the liberal arts college, specifically language and literature ("poetry"), history, and philosophy. Those disciplines allow "the critical discovery of our own nature by use of the most reliable evidence and the most accurate ways available to treat it."

But these three studies could not meet all the student's needs. Other studies must complement them. "History, poetry, and philosophy, which view man from within and according to the law for man, give a partial account of our nature unless supplemented and criticized by the study of externals—the nature of human groups and of the physical world." The curriculum, then, must prominently include social studies and science. But Chalmers warns against the social sciences being taught as others had advocated and as he observed in the practices of the universities: "… to the student who knows nothing but social sciences, man is known only by his function or participation in the group. If man himself is most notable because he is a member of a social institution, no matter how exalted the institution, he is already a slave." Were Chalmers proposing a curriculum design, it is clear, study of the social sciences would be built upon the foundation of study in the humanities.

The sciences must play their vital part: "The cultivation of the scientific mind is of the highest importance in liberal education ... basic to thinking because of extensive use to the mind wherever it confronts the mysteries of the physical world." But again Chalmers is suspicious of contemporary practice, particularly of inquiry in the sciences being unconstrained. He sees the need for the study of the sciences to be limited and influenced by knowledge of and adherence to the humanities, lest science become only technology or dangerous generalization.

All of this keen, disciplined engagement with the central, vital studies to what purpose? Not, as some apologists for liberal education have argued, to produce Platonic observers of life in detachment. Not to conclude that these are "useless" activities, ornamental, ephemeral. Not to permit faculty members to create young humanists, social scientists, or scientists in their own image and pack them off to graduate school. The purpose, "the end[,] of liberal education is commitment and action." It was painful for Chalmers to recognize how little respect for liberal education there was in those universities where training towards a profession had become paramount and where liberal studies were seen as avoidance of commitment to "serious" study. "The critical subjects are now distinctly regarded as luxurious; in large sections of higher education the liberal student of science, the humanities, or society is dismissed as one marking time until ... he can make up his mind about a calling." Fifty years later that view is, sadly, entrenched.

In his final paragraph Chalmers returns us to the place where he began, his belief in the education of individuals to the sense of their responsibility for their freedom and for the Republic: "It cannot be too often repeated that nothing is more certain in modern society than that the continuance of the Republic is based on the quality of the individual and his education as a person, and that liberty is based upon a belief in and understanding of the moral law." Thomas Jefferson might have written that sentence.

I have always found compelling in *The Republic and the Person* the author's underlying faith in the capacity of students and teachers alike to deal with the great central issues of our world. He knew full well that this demands much of both, particularly a commitment to rigorous study and to each other. The best form of learning, Chalmers maintained, came when the student did a great deal of writing and the teacher spent much time in writing commentary on the student's work. And the best kind of teaching came when the faculty member spoke out of a conviction which went beyond a mastery of subject matter and authority in the discipline. One sentence in particular makes clear why Chalmers thought his prime responsibility as President to be the recruitment of faculty members: "I fail to see how one can teach well, except according to his idea, however hazy, halting, and tentative, of the ultimate purpose of life." That, of course, no program of graduate study can provide in and of itself, whether it is undertaken at Oxford, Harvard, or Ohio State.

There emerges out of Chalmers's thinking an image of a triangle, at the points of which are student, teacher, and essential studies; within that triangle all that is important in liberal education will take place. But the key, clearly, as many references in Chalmers's text make clear, is the character of the professor. "The key question about any college is how large a fraction of its scholars, scientists, and teachers are committed to the central inquiry concerning man in the universe and what portion of those understand the peculiarly human terms of the problem. If the portion is large, the education pursued is likely to be liberal."

When I was invited to join the faculty of Kenyon College, I imagined that I would find there a place where I could teach language and literature out of my own convictions about the worth of their study, where I could do for my students what Willem Graff had done for me at McGill. President Chalmers, I soon learned, expected me to *educate* my students and to do my teaching out of a sense of the College's great purpose.

At some point in my English schooldays, when I read eagerly about all things French and in particular about Paris, I came on an account of an English couple visiting that city. They were fearful that, walking about the streets unescorted in pursuit of the France they wanted so much to embrace, they would get lost. "Do not worry," the concierge at their hotel told them. "In Paris there is the Eiffel Tower. You can always get your bearings from that." For Kenyon, Gordon Chalmers was the Eiffel Tower. He was the leader who had brought Kenyon into the first rank of America's colleges by being the spokesman for a purposeful form of education, the accomplished publicist for crucial ideas, the model of the teacher/scholar, the visionary. That was the Chalmers the world beyond Gambier knew—the College's alumni, his peers in the academy, those in the general public who were interested in education. We who were members of the College recognized that from him, we could always get our bearings.

Chapter IV
The Chalmers Kenyon

We didn't have to serve time in the barracks after all. We were invited to live in a furnished apartment in one of the two brand-new freshmen dormitories, which were outside the College Park. After some years of damaging academic failures in the freshmen classes, Chalmers had decided to separate the freshmen from the temptations of life in the upper-class residences. Gretchen and I, the letter from Dean Bailey said, would provide an adult presence in the building—a presumably stabilizing influence—and I would be resident counselor. The promise of free utilities and three hundred dollars added to my salary was enough, after seven years of bare-bones living, to overcome any doubts we had.

Before that we had been startled one Sunday morning in May to find President Chalmers at our door. At Harvard for a meeting, he had thought to stop by—"an opportunity to meet Mrs. Haywood," as he explained smiling. Only after Bailey's letter came did we understand that his meeting Gretchen was to allow him to make sure she would fit the role he imagined for her. I was impressed again at the care he was willing to take to make sure he had the people he wanted.

We stayed in Norton Hall for five years, partly because, being childless, we were low on the totem pole when faculty housing units became available. It was an apprenticeship I have always been glad I served, for I had the opportunity to get to know young Americans and their mores far more quickly than I would otherwise have done. I learned a great deal about Kenyon from the freshmen's reactions to it, even as I learned how they assessed their courses and the work that was expected of them. It was mid-September, two weeks after our arrival in Gambier, before I saw Chalmers again. It was in the Church of the Holy Spirit, at the formal Opening of College, which we of the faculty and the members of the freshman class were required to attend. There was an academic procession, one of five in the course of the year. Even with the presence of the faculty from the seminary the line was short. The faculty of the College that year numbered just over thirty: a dozen in mathematics and the sciences; eight in history, political science, economics; a dozen in the humanities, with Classics having but one member, my department four, philosophy three, and English five, which made it the largest in the College. The arts were scarcely evident, there being a full-time member in drama, one man in music who was shared with the seminary, a part-timer in art. The chaplain, who taught in the seminary, taught the sole course in religion at the

College. Not one member of the full-time faculty was a female, Kenyon being so emphatically all-male that, when some years later I asked the trustees to allow wives of faculty and staff members to *audit* courses, they declared that the presence of women would "destroy the ambience of the classroom." Kenyon's official occasions in those days were appropriately formal. The tone set at them seemed to support the President's claim that here serious work was done. After a hymn and some words from the deans, Chalmers spoke from the pulpit, his voice firm and strong. He told the freshmen what the College expected of them; his emphasis throughout was on rigor, on what was demanded. The students were there to work and, under the guidance of their professors, to become liberally educated. As we left the church there was a murmur among the junior faculty beside me, voices approving the President's message.

    Before that day I had met the large majority of the faculty and I was impressed by them, not only because the Catalogue told me of their holding doctoral degrees from some of the world's best universities, but because of their lively interest in me and in what I hoped to do at the College. It was easy to have such contacts in Ascension Hall, for people kept their doors open. Some, seeing me in my office in those early days, looked in to introduce themselves; some were brought to my office door by Ed Harvey, my colleague in French, from whom I quickly learned how different were the expectations of faculty members at Kenyon from those he and I had known at Harvard. Eventually I was to learn how many of the faculty had resigned university positions in order to be at a college where teaching was of first priority. As I was doing, they had come to Kenyon to seek the ironically broader horizons in the small college that were created by ongoing dialogue among colleagues. One who came a few years after me, an associate professor of economics, told me that he had fled Ohio State because his daily round brought him into contact only with other economists. He was housed and did his teaching in a building occupied only by his department; he lunched with colleagues of the department; he parked his car, he said with heavy irony, in a lot reserved for economists. Like him, I relished the opportunity to talk to members of other departments, including those in the sciences. One of my early friends was a member of Chemistry, a Canadian who had spent a post-doc year doing research in England. Like so many of his colleagues in that division he was broadly educated and broadly interested. There was nothing about him of the scientist who retreats into the lab and shuts himself off from human intercourse. It was he and those like him who really made the Chalmers Kenyon work, professors who, as Chalmers put it, were "committed to the central inquiry concerning man in the universe" and who understood "the peculiarly human terms of the problem."

The fact was that the members of the Kenyon faculty saw a great deal of one another. Not only was there constant exchange in the halls of academic buildings and, for some of us who sought it, over midmorning coffee in the basement of Peirce Hall, there was also a remarkable amount of faculty socialization at Friday afternoon cocktail hours. I never learned whether Chalmers had specifically encouraged it, but it was quickly clear to me that senior members thought it their responsibility to create social gatherings where colleagues, particularly the juniors, could talk to one another. Nearly always, it seemed to me, the talk was of Kenyon matters and of what people were doing in their work. I had a host of valuable exchanges with colleagues and their wives. I was learning just how important was collegiality to the success of a liberal arts college, how crucial the open and constant interest in one another's professional activity.

Collegiality and communication are not givens in a college. Small size does not guarantee that there will be exchanges among members of the faculty or between the faculty and the administrators. In some of the consultancies I did, I found small colleges where there were yawning gulfs between the academic divisions and even between departments within divisions. At a Lutheran college with some sixty faculty members, I asked a long-serving professor of religion when he had last had a conversation on a college matter with a member of the philosophy department. He thought for a moment and said, "Would you believe never?" The faculty members in that institution were almost totally ignorant of the work being done in other departments.

Just as there are those in small colleges who believe that no great teaching goes on in universities, so there are some in universities who believe that there is no research done in small colleges. My eyes were quickly opened in my first months to the amount of research being done by members of the Kenyon faculty: Charles Coffin was writing a book on John Donne, Charles Thornton was doing research on limb regeneration in salamanders, Virgil Aldrich was working hard at publications on aesthetics, Charles Ritcheson and Landon Warner on books on English and American history respectively. Everybody in the science division seemed to have summer grants from the National Science Foundation. There were others, known in their fields for their published work, for their papers at professional meetings, for the part they played in the development of the Advanced Placement Program. Then there were men like Denham Sutcliffe, scholars in the fullest sense, who published little, but were constantly at work on research which translated into new and deeper insights they brought before their students in the classroom. Sad to say, "scholarship" has become a synonym for "publication" and in most institutions today "scholar" is a title reserved for somebody who is appearing regularly in print. Harvey informed me early that Chalmers expected to see faculty members continuing to grow in their discipline and that promotion to full professor came only after a faculty member had published a book or had made an equal contribution in his discipline. What the very large majority of the faculty of that time had in common was their sense that they owed it to their students to be working in their discipline, keeping themselves abreast of what was newly important in their fields.

But the first priority was teaching and every member of the faculty taught; the editor of the *Review* taught a course on poetry each semester, Dean Bailey taught a course in history. The standard "load" was four courses in each semester—with classes on Saturday mornings as well—a standard I exceeded in my first couple of years as I sought to handle elementary and intermediate language courses besides developing literature courses for my first majors. There were two of them waiting eagerly for my arrival. Besides my courses and the time I had to give to Norton Hall when the College was in session, I was immediately assigned to the faculty committees on admissions and athletics. And then there was my still not completed dissertation, which claimed me on Sundays and on every vacation day until, happily, I was done.

Being busy, busy, busy was the ordinary condition of the Kenyon faculty member. But I didn't hear complaints. People loved their work. They were proud to be at Kenyon, secure in the knowledge that their institution counted for something in higher education. They didn't need to apologize to their friends in the Ivy League for the choice they had made. My colleagues talked constantly of their students, whom they knew intimately from the work those students turned in or in working side by side with them in labs and studios. The intimacy was not the phony stuff of today, called that because students call professors by their first names, hug them after class, or smoke pot with them. It was the intimacy that comes through working at shared ideas, from the give and take of discussion of important questions, from having mutual respect. One of the things I came to value most about Kenyon was that I had students over the full four years, watched them grow, saw them mature into intellectuals and men. Not all of them did, of course. It was possible, even in Chalmers's lifetime, for a student to scrape through with a low-C average, though it was not the Kenyon style for a student to boast that he was doing that.

Once I got used to there being no women, I found Kenyon's student body an intriguing mix. I once heard a colleague complain that there were too many preppies in the student body, to which Denham Sutcliffe responded in characteristic fashion, "The children of the very rich are as deserving of liberal education as the children of the very poor." My best students were the equal of any I had at Harvard, but the bottom of Kenyon's freshman class went down deeper than Harvard's. There were students at Kenyon from very wealthy families; there were children of middle-class parents who were stretching to pay the costs; and there were some who were there on scholarships. The faculty often said of Chalmers that he spent money on the right things and they were unanimous in approving his commitment to leavening the student body by bringing in talented students on generous scholarships. One of the worst setbacks for

Kenyon in later years was its being forced by its near bankruptcy to reduce its scholarship program significantly.

The very large majority in the student body came from the east coast, where the idea of separate colleges for men and women still held sway. Kenyon was the only men's college in Ohio, which led the director of admissions to call it "an eastern college geographically misplaced," and there was an abiding conviction among most members of the College that the all-male character fostered hard work and solid learning. But my position on the admissions committee soon let me understand that getting bright young men to come to an all-male college in isolated, rural Ohio was no easy thing. The director of admissions spent many weeks every year touring the eastern prep schools and the best public high schools between Philadelphia and Boston. There, at least, he had a friendly reception, thanks to Chalmers's reputation, but in co-ed Ohio it was increasingly difficult for the admissions office to convince the best students. Oberlin and Antioch, Ohio colleges that were generally thought Kenyon's equal academically, could offer female companions without thirty or forty miles of driving home after a date. By the mid-fifties Kenyon was having to work hard to meet its enrollment goals, while its financial circumstances sometimes forced it to retain upper-class students it might otherwise have dropped for poor scholarship. I remember a tense moment in my very first year at Kenyon. It came early in a fall faculty meeting, when President Chalmers announced that he had reinstated five of the six students who had been dropped by the committee on academic standing; the College, he said, could not afford the loss of their fees. There was no protest from the faculty; his colleagues were plainly embarrassed for Chalmers that he had felt compelled to make the ruling. Kenyon would know more such moments before it finally achieved financial stability.

Those students who hoped to go on to medical school, law school, or other graduate study could be confident in Kenyon's reputation to open doors for them. The College had a remarkable record of success. From that tiny undergraduate body there were three Rhodes Scholars in my first few years; students entered the country's best medical and law schools and thrived there; in the lifespan of the Woodrow Wilson Fellowship Program, when winners were given support for their first year of graduate study in the arts and sciences, Kenyon had the highest percentage of winners in the Michigan/Ohio region. It was both the College's reputation for rigor and its unwavering commitment to liberal education that helped bring those students through to success.

Even as Chalmers expected maturity in students in the classroom, he wished to count on it in their extra-classroom life. Upper-class students, all of them housed in the residence halls on the Hill, as the south end of the Park was always called, lived without direct supervision. There were no proctors in those halls, no assistant deans watching over them. Bailey was the College's only dean, serving faculty and students alike (though Chalmers took unto himself most of the responsibility for the faculty), helped by just one assistant, a recent graduate of the College who maintained communications between Bailey and the fraternities. In those days about ninety percent of the students belonged to fraternities, both national and local, all of them occupying vertical divisions of the upper-class residences. There were no separate houses. During the week, the evidence seemed to show, most upperclassmen were busy with their studies and the halls were relatively orderly. But Saturdays were party time, at least in the parlors of the national fraternities. The two local fraternities, which sought to attract the most able students into membership, were more tranquil. If women were to be present at parties, there had to be faculty members and their spouses present as chaperons. Younger faculty were regularly called to that duty and on the whole, in those years before thumping stereos, it was a pleasant experience.

There was drinking at those parties and Kenyon was notorious all over Ohio because it was the only college that allowed its students to drink on campus. Ohio permitted eighteen-year-olds to drink three-two beer, so called because the percentage of alcohol in it was less than 3.2% (in contrast to the six percent of the regular brew), and Chalmers ruled that students should exercise their legal rights on campus. He was more concerned for the students than for public image: better that students should stay at home and drink, to be able to fall into bed if they had too much, than to drink in town and be out on the highway afterwards. Chalmers was well aware, as was everybody else, that at neighboring institutions the students, chased off campus by the "dry" rule there, drove to the next town and had parties in rented hotel rooms. So it was at colleges and universities all over the State of Ohio. But Kenyon's honesty on the issue brought it no applause. In 1955 I went down to Columbus to my first meeting of the Ohio Chapter of the American Association of Teachers of German, where I was accosted during the coffee hour before business started by a faculty member from the University of

Cincinnati. Reading my name tag and noting my Kenyon identity, he looked up with a leer and asked, "Is it true that your students come to class drunk?" I came up with a great retort, but only when I was driving home.

I am confident that President Chalmers was as disappointed by student failure to mature into responsible social behavior as he was by failure to mature intellectually. But on both counts, I am equally confident, Kenyon had far more success than it had failure. How often have I heard from the College's alumni expressions of gratitude that Kenyon forced them to stretch their mental capacities, to work hard, and to accept responsibility. For some, and I have been in touch with them too, Kenyon socially was a prolonged agony, but they stuck it out because of the great teachers they had.

Those teachers were not—I think of the Rhodes Scholarship phrase again—mere "laureates of the classroom." I have written earlier of their scholarship and their professional reputations beyond Gambier. But they were also tireless workers on Kenyon's behalf, taking on committee assignments, meeting with student groups, advising fraternities, and supporting student activities in the theater, the newspaper, and athletics. There was a remarkable intensity about Kenyon life in those days. Every Tuesday morning at eleven there was an assembly, which students were required to attend and which members of the faculty attended out of a sense of duty. Speakers on those occasions were often brought in from elsewhere, but more often than not it was the President or another faculty member who spoke. Then there were some Sunday afternoons—yes, Sunday—in the Archon lounge, when that local fraternity invited faculty members to speak on whatever topics they chose. Like fraternity parties on Saturday night, the Archon gathering was open to everybody and a large number of people invariably turned out. Such hours contributed greatly to the building of the sense of membership in a community of scholars.

Any attempt to say why the Chalmers Kenyon worked so well must note the fact of its single focus on the life of the College whenever it was in session. Many observers have noted that Chalmers seemed to prefer to have faculty members who were English or who had studied in England. Certainly the number of such persons in Gambier could not have been arrived at accidentally. But I am convinced that Chalmers did not consider a Harvard doctorate inferior to an Oxford degree or American intellectuals less than English. What he sought, I believe, were men who had embraced the English university idea of a single focus upon learning, the subordination of private interest to the collegiate, the priority of rigorous study over all else. (It was difficult for me, in my early days in this country, to accept the idea of students having jobs during the semester, particularly when I learned that most of those who did were working to support their automobiles and driver's insurance.) Yes, there was also in the Chalmers world a place for athletics, but not in the forefront of college life; a time for socializing, but never to the degree that it distracted from a college's purpose. How Chalmers would have lamented the findings of a study in the nineteen-eighties, which reported that the large majority of American students chose their college on what it offered by way of social life. He would not have considered that Kenyon, any more than Oxford, was responsible for long-term healthcare for students or for their feeling happy. Least of all would he have thought that the College owed its students entertainment. Though he may not have shared Philander Chase's view that the larger world would inevitably corrupt his students, Chalmers was certainly convinced that the larger world would *distract* them from their studies.

The ultimate focus of Kenyon life was, of course, the classroom. The range of subject matters offered to students then would seem laughably limited to most observers today. To prevent premature specialization, the requirements for the degree set limits on the amount of course work a student could take in a major program; consequently, there was less pressure than there would be today to add to course offerings. Instead there was an emphasis on students having a common experience in the curriculum and within departmental offerings. The most celebrated course at Kenyon in those years was the year-long freshman English course. Sections of it, each having a dozen or fifteen students, were taught by all the members of the Department, using a common syllabus and texts. I continue to find great value in the idea of having all freshmen reading *Huckleberry Finn* or *Paradise Lost* at the same time; there is much to be said also for the kind of faculty discussion that preceded agreement on the choice of texts. Similar practices ruled in the first courses in history, political science, philosophy, and other subjects, with the result that I, teaching a course on Goethe and his contemporaries, say, could confidently allude to what students had covered in those courses. It was always interesting to me, too, to find the subject matters of those courses entering into faculty conversations at Friday afternoon cocktail parties; they were the whole faculty's subject matter.

Few things can better illustrate the sense of faculty involvement in the total curriculum than the processes that governed the introduction of a new course. The instructor had first to get the backing of his department before the proposed new course advanced to the division meeting. There questions were asked about the subject matter and its appropriateness to the liberal arts curriculum, as well as about the implications for staffing, teaching hours, availability of library materials and the like. With the division's blessing the course went to the curriculum committee, chaired by the Dean, where it would be championed by the division's representative. I know at first hand how searching were the questions at both the division and committee levels. But that was not the end. The Dean brought a recommendation then to the faculty meeting and there was always a period of questioning from the floor before a vote was called. By the time approval was granted, a new course had been thoroughly scrutinized and every member in the meeting knew what was intended in that course. I remember so very clearly, as though I were seeing a crack in the foundation of Ascension Hall, the first challenge to that process voiced by a member of the faculty. It was in 1964, not long after I had become Dean, when I offered for the faculty's discussion a proposed new course in political science. I had scarcely sat down when an associate professor of English, recently arrived from Yale, rose and offered objection. "I am a specialist on seventeenth-century English literature," he proclaimed. "I don't know anything about political science and I don't want to. I can't vote intelligently on this. I shouldn't be expected to. The whole thing's a farce." We didn't know it then, but we were hearing the voice that announced the beginning of the end. Within the year that same member was demanding that he be allowed to choose his own texts for his section of freshman English.

But in the Kenyon of Gordon Chalmers, no such voice was heard; consensus still prevailed. We thought it our responsibility to know enough about our colleagues' work to be able to understand what was involved in the introduction of new courses, in evaluating candidates for the degree with honors, in providing input, when we were asked, on the merits of a colleague up for promotion or tenure. Those things seemed obviously the responsibility of the faculty, that body which we thought the most essential element in a college that prized the essentials. That Kenyon's financial resources were very limited was known to everybody. But its intellectual, human resources, we thought, were remarkable. There was profound agreement among us that our students were working at the right subjects, that the curriculum was properly weighted to ensure that students had a broad context of understanding into which to place their special interest, their major. There was a great deal of mutual respect which manifested itself in common courtesies and attention to what people said in faculty meetings. The character of those meetings, at four o' clock on Monday afternoon once a month, has always seemed to me emblematic of the collegiality of the place.

The faculty met in the Campbell-Meeker Room, a lovely paneled space in Ascension Hall which was an anteroom to the President's chambers. We took our places in large comfortable chairs arranged in some half dozen rows of five or six seats. There was quiet talk until four o'clock struck. At that moment Dean Bailey, satisfied that all of us were present, knocked on the President's closed door and Chalmers entered the room. The faculty rose and remained standing until he was seated. That set the tone for meetings which, while they sometimes saw passionate statements and hard questioning, were always assemblies of professionals doing their work. The petty and the personal had no place there. We were gathered to do the business of the College.

Chapter V
Leadership Lost

Gordon Chalmers was not universally admired. Though nobody doubted his integrity or his intellectual strengths, he had his critics in the alumni and trustee bodies. Even among the faculty there were one or two who thought that he did not consult the faculty enough or believed that he was not attentive enough to contrary views that might be offered him. It was alleged that he had appointed the bachelor member of Philosophy without consulting the department and had even, in some distant past, brought in a chairman to one department without the incumbent having any notion that he was being replaced. Then there were older alumni who, reportedly, would not contribute to the College's support, either with their money or in persuading students to attend, because they believed Chalmers had made Kenyon "too intellectual." More importantly, impatience with Chalmers had grown among the trustees, who faulted him for not being a better administrator. After his death we heard that some trustees were offended by the President's having made expensive commitments without their prior approval. The board members were particularly concerned about the mounting deficit and the deteriorating physical plant.

Kenyon's fundamental problem was that its ambitions far outstripped its ability to fund them. Poor by any financial criterion, Kenyon was seeking to match the achievements of colleges that ranked amongst the wealthiest in the country, particularly in terms of endowment dollars per student. Always a measuring rod for Kenyon, Amherst College could boast of a library with its own endowment larger than Kenyon's entire endowment. One could call Kenyon "a miracle on a shoestring," as one of my friends liked to do, but it was living on the edge of the abyss.

Most of this was not known to the faculty in Chalmers's lifetime. When it had been said that Chalmers was not an effective fund raiser, his defenders had been quick to point out that he was very successful, in fact, in getting foundation support for his projects: from Ford and Carnegie, for example, for the founding of *The Kenyon Review* and the conferences that were so important in getting the College's name before the public. But it was known, at the same time, that foundation support for the literary journal had not been continued, once the *Review* was established. The faculty's concerns had to do with Kenyon's salaries lagging behind those at neighboring colleges, inadequate housing, and the obvious need for new laboratory equipment and physical plant maintenance. But even those anxieties did not diminish the admiration and esteem the vast majority of the faculty offered Chalmers.

It was not surprising, then, that after the first shock of his death the faculty should quickly agree that what Kenyon needed in his office was a man with all of Chalmers's powers, but also the management skills he was thought to lack and an ability to raise money for current operations. There was general agreement that there was no such man at the College; Frank Bailey, quickly named by the board to be acting president for a year, had many friends among the faculty, but he was never thought a candidate.

Given the choice the trustees eventually made, it seems evident that they were almost exclusively concerned to have a president who could bring financial stability to the College and deal with the deferred maintenance and other pressing needs. The faculty were not invited to have representatives on the trustees' search committee and the man selected did not appear in Gambier until after he had been appointed. The new President was Franze Edward Lund, who liked to be called "Buck."

In most faculty minds Lund was such a disaster that he was never given credit for the physical plant improvements that were made during his tenure. They were significant: a chemistry building in 1962; a third freshman dorm in '63; an extension to the dining room in '64; two new upper-class residences in '66. Just as important to Kenyon's future was Lund's recognition that the seminary had become not only a drain on the College's resources, but, with marked decline in the quality of its student body, an embarrassing partner to have. He proposed a separation, which was achieved with remarkable absence of rancor and no schism with the Episcopal Church, as the seminary moved off to Rochester, New York, in an ecumenical grouping of seminaries. The great credit for the final accord belongs to the man who was to succeed Lund, a trustee and alumnus who skillfully negotiated a settlement. When William G. Caples met with the College faculty to inform us of the settlement, he was given a standing ovation. There was a sense of a great burden having been lifted off our collective shoulders and the potential for a new life for Kenyon.

The happiest achievement of the Lund years was the building of a new library. Chalmers had long before recognized the pressing need for a much larger facility and he had worked with architects in 1948 to develop plans; they were consumed, so to speak, in the Old Kenyon fire. What seemed to us a splendid new library was finished and dedicated in 1962 and, most happily, named for President Chalmers. His old friend Robert Frost spoke at the dedication, describing the library as "a sanctuary of the humanities, a stronghold of the humanities. And a place of resort for students—young people, older people, but young people particularly, who are having it out with themselves about God and man and sociology and poetry ...." I am certain Chalmers would have been delighted by those words, which might have been said equally about his Kenyon College. The Chalmers Library today is lost to view from Middle Path, concealed by a much larger and more conspicuous Olin Library. I have found its subordination more than a little symbolic. It was several years after that dedication that Lund told me that the trustees of the College had misled him at the time of his appointment. Before he accepted the position, he claimed, the trustees assured him that he would have little more than a figurehead role at Kenyon. The academic program was well established and much respected; Kenyon's fame would guarantee a steady flow of students; the trustees themselves "would take care of the financial end." Lund's early behavior in office would certainly confirm that such was his belief.

One can readily find in Lund's history facts which would argue to the trustees that he was the man to lead Kenyon, given their sense of the

College's first needs. The son of Episcopal missionaries, he had grown up in China before earning a degree at Washington and Lee, a respected liberal arts college in Virginia. He had served as professor, dean of the college, and finally President of Alabama College, a small college for women that he had evidently brought to financial health through expanding its student body and making it coeducational. For most of the faculty those facts were not impressive; nobody had heard of Alabama College. That his Ph.D. was neither Ivy League nor Oxford did not help his cause. That was enough for some to wonder, even before he appeared on campus, whether he was an intellectual match for his office. His first addresses to the Kenyon community sadly suggested that he was not.

He did not get off to a good start, though the fault for that was scarcely his. The Faculty Council decided that there should be a welcoming banquet for the new President and his wife and that the faculty's most distinguished member—and a fellow Southerner—was the appropriate person to speak the faculty's welcome. John Crowe Ransom startled his colleagues by issuing, in effect, a warning to Lund that he must not expect to lead Kenyon, for the leadership of the College was in the hands of the faculty. Denham Sutcliffe and I turned to look at each other, our faces registering our astonishment and disbelief. The Lunds looked both ill at ease and bewildered. Ransom was held in such esteem that, to the best of my knowledge, nobody ever asked him about his address or what inspired it. It made a deep impression on Buck Lund. He stumbled through a response and he told me years later that he believed Ransom's every word, even as he believed the trustees when they told him they would be responsible for the College's finances. So, as the faculty waited for Lund to lead them in the Chalmers fashion, Lund waited for the leadership from the faculty Ransom had assured him would come.

Long after any respect I might have had for Lund had vanished, he told me that he had come to Kenyon expecting to be able "to put his feet up," after having had "a very tough life" as professor, dean, and president; he resented being labeled a do-nothing president. Yet it was easy to see him as that. He was scarcely visible at the College. He walked to his office on weekdays at about eleven in the morning and stayed there only long enough to check his mail and sign letters before returning to Cromwell Cottage at about one. He was frank to tell me that he kept such hours because he didn't want to be bothered by people dropping into his office; he believed the faculty and the students would be at lunch then. He did return on Monday afternoons at four for meetings of the Faculty Council (which he chaired), and for monthly faculty meetings, but his performance then ranged from the defensive to the petulant. That his first official action after his arrival was to appoint a Dean of Students, leaving Bailey free to deal only with the faculty, told us that faculty matters would no longer be in the President's hands. Further, it was soon rumored that Lund was making no effort to raise money for the College's operations; he was said to resist going out to alumni meetings after his first forays had alumni audiences giving him a cool reception. Denham Sutcliffe, a man who, like me, needed a president he could respect, did his best to find virtues in Lund. He took him rabbit hunting so as to have opportunity to offer him advice and guidance. To Lund's ever-growing body of critics Sutcliffe offered defense by pointing to the Chalmers Library and other physical plant improvements. But the poverty of Lund's addresses to the College, his obviously low energy levels, and his self-indulgent conduct of his office were too much in the end even for kindly Sutcliffe. What I heard from my Norton Hall freshmen added to my anxieties. Quick to pick up on the negative comparisons with Chalmers the upperclassmen made in their presence, the freshmen echoed criticism of Lund, while the College newspaper became ever more vocal in its denunciations of the President. It was probably in 1960 that Sutcliffe, who had by then told me that he had lost all confidence in Dean Bailey's ability to lead the faculty, observed, "I think the College could survive Frank Bailey. I think the College could survive Buck Lund. But I don't believe the College can survive the combination of the two of them." We were both increasingly anxious about Kenyon and the loss of the center that Gordon Chalmers had provided.

The first years of Lund's presidency found me so busy with my own work that I had neither time for, nor much interest in, the College's larger problems. Things were going extraordinarily well for me. In the year that Chalmers died, Harvard invited me to adapt my dissertation for publication as the first volume in a new series of Harvard Germanic Studies. I had become involved with the Advanced Placement Program's German section. Enrollments in German courses expanded by leaps and bounds, and I was able to convince the Dean to engage a second man, the native German partner I had imagined when I was first appointed. Though I began to feel the anxieties of my colleagues mounting, I wasn't ready to think, as some of them were already thinking, that Kenyon was not a place to make a career.

A particular reason for negative thinking became evident in the aftermath of a visit from a representative of the Ford Foundation. At that time Ford was very much interested in higher education and most particularly in its future, as "going to college" became increasingly the thing for young Americans to plan for. Citing the evidence of crowded classrooms in the country's elementary and secondary schools, Ford foresaw severe enrollment pressures on public universities, and argued that the private colleges should take their share of the "rising tide," not simply seek to become more and more selective. To encourage private colleges to consider significant expansion, Ford offered grants of a million dollars and more to institutions that would show plans for a doubling of their size. Such growth, in Ford's view, could only benefit the colleges as demand grew for modern facilities and equipment.

The Foundation sent one of its staff to Kenyon, though not at the College's invitation. I was invited to be one of a small group of faculty members to meet with the representative in Lund's living room. I was there in my capacity as chair of the admissions committee, a position I held for several years until I became Dean and which directly acquainted me with the mounting problems of getting the good students the College wanted and—almost desperately—

needed. The Ford man was well rehearsed and the meeting was not a comfortable one. We found ourselves called on to answer questions which demanded of us more knowledge than we had of the College's operations. Lund often interrupted to remark that the questions were not really relevant to Kenyon, since there was no thought in Gambier of major expansion.

As we broke up, the Ford representative invited me to have breakfast with him the following morning. I accepted, of course, but not eagerly; the evening had made me apprehensive. After quizzing me about numbers of applicants and numbers admitted, he took me aback by saying, "Your president is obviously not a leader and I can't imagine you get any academic leadership from your Dean. Where does leadership come from here?" I mumbled a hastily improvised answer, talking of Chalmers and his legacy, but the visitor's expression told me that it was hopelessly inadequate. He left Gambier with Lund having told him that Kenyon would entertain no plans for growth beyond seven hundred students; we were well content to be what we were.

In 1957 I became an American citizen, something neither my wife nor Kenyon had demanded of me. I recognized that the time had come for me to make the change when I found myself using "we" and meaning "we Americans." I asked my first two majors, then seniors, to accompany Gretchen and me to the ceremony. It was a day I had every reason to rejoice in.

In 1959 we left Norton Hall, my seniority now being such that I was able to claim a small house being vacated by the Professor of Classics. He took advantage of a changed circumstance at the College. With the time having come to demolish the sagging barracks and with the College short on housing, the trustees declared that a faculty member might, in lieu of housing supplied by the College, have an additional thousand dollars in salary and find his own housing. However, such housing had to be within five miles of the Gambier post office; that was soon called "the five-mile rule." Three years later, after the midwinter meeting of the trustees, President Lund announced an even more drastic change. The federal tax law, which had to that point made tax-exempt the housing of those who were living in properties owned by their employer, was changed to exempt only those who had to live in a particular property in order to perform the work of their office. Henceforth, then, the faculty would not be housed "at the pleasure of the College" and instead would have their salaries increased by 18% and provide their own housing. Moreover, the College would at once offer for sale to those occupying them its houses which were outside the College Park.

Only with the advantage of hindsight can one recognize the significance of the College's giving up the Philander Chase idea of a faculty in residence, so crucial to the Chalmers Kenyon's notion of the single focus on the life of the College. At the time, though, the change made little difference, for there were houses and apartments available for rent in Gambier and only the Classics professor moved out into the country.

By this time I had been taken under the wing of two senior professors who, in every sense, became my mentors. So far as I know, there was no official system at the College of senior faculty serving as mentors to juniors, but newcomers seemed to find their way into the care of at least one senior member. I couldn't have been more fortunate in the two men who became my friends and my teachers.

Virgil Aldrich, twenty years my senior, was one of the most disciplined thinkers I have ever known and a great teacher. He and his colleague in Philosophy, Phil Rice, had attracted a remarkably large and fine group of students to their discipline; in my first couple of years at Kenyon there were more majors in philosophy than in any other department. (Rice was killed in a car wreck in my second year, before I got to know him.) My move, at the beginning of my third year, from the top floor of Ascension to the basement put me on the same floor as Aldrich, and he promptly invited me in for a chat. He had a first reason for being interested in me; he had married a Swiss German. I quickly found reason for being interested in him and I often walked down the corridor to his office to talk. Whenever I think of Virgil, it is in his office that I place him, for he seemed always to be there, often until very late in the evening. And always he was working at his texts. I sometimes found him gazing hard at a wall, as though he might pull out of its plaster an answer to the question he was wrestling with. But it was not difficult to draw him away from that and into conversation of the kind I wanted with him. He was the most gentle of men, never letting me think that my question was as foolish as it was; he gave it a weight it didn't deserve. In Aldrich I found the man to whom I could always carry a question, engrossed though he was with his work. He was one of those on the faculty who, while they were always engaged with scholarship, published little. But in later years when I visited colleges as a consultant, I found professors of philosophy at once associating Kenyon with Aldrich. "I know his work on aesthetics, of course," was the characteristic comment. One of the more painful days in my life came, years later, when Aldrich, already into his 'sixties, came to my office to tell me that he had decided to leave. He had come to a point, he said, where his interests demanded that he confine his teaching to graduate students and that was what he would do for the few years that remained to his career. I felt his loss as much for myself as I did for the College; he could not be replaced.

But more important to me ultimately was Denham Sutcliffe, in part because I had more in common with him than I had with Aldrich. This was "Denham Sutcliffe, Bookseller," as the sign outside his little shop proclaimed him; the bookstore was where he spent his Sundays until, finally, he sold off his stock, admitting that he couldn't afford to go on losing money. Sutcliffe was closer to me in age, twelve years older, and we taught kindred subject matters. But we had some common roots besides. Sutcliffe was conceived in my native Yorkshire, born in Pennsylvania, and returned as a babe-in-arms to Yorkshire when his suddenly widowed mother could not support herself here. For his first seven years he and his mother lived with her sisters in a bleak mill town, less than thirty miles from my village. A second husband took his mother and him to Maine, exchanging one country's poverty for another's. He and I had mothers who told us that being a good student was the only way to avoid working in the factory or the coal mine, fathers who were either at work or too tired to have much to do with us. While at Oxford Sutcliffe made only one visit to his aunts in Yorkshire; it was an unhappy affair for all of them and he never went back. But he retained an affection for his early years there and I could always make him laugh by lapsing into the dialect that was his first language and mine.

Sutcliffe was the only member of the Kenyon faculty who was Gordon Chalmers's intellectual equal. He was elected a Rhodes Scholar at twenty-four, having had to drop out of Bates College for two years to work in a shoe factory to earn enough money to support his last two years. He had a brilliant career at Oxford, earning first class honors in English, a nearly unheard-of feat for an American in those days, and being invited to stay on to take a doctorate. The beginning of the war in 1939 caused him to be sent home, together with all American students, and he completed his degree *in absentia*. There was much that he always valued about Oxford, but he was as appalled as Chalmers had been by the political naiveté he had seen there. Sutcliffe was first, foremost, and always an American, deeply engaged with the literature and history of this country, believing always that it would more likely be destroyed from within than without. He was a sometimes-angry Democrat, brimming with hostility to the English class system his mother had never been able to escape, affronted by a world in which there was desperate poverty.

The College had no orator to match Sutcliffe. He was the best platform speaker I have ever heard, and his assembly addresses were always the year's highlight. It was he who introduced the freshmen to the College and its purpose, addressing them formally after the first dinner they ate in Peirce Hall on the day of their arrival. He inspired awe in them and, I suspect, expectations of their professors that we weren't all able to match. As a teacher he had no peer.

It was in the summer after Chalmers died that I first approached Sutcliffe. Before then I had heeded warning from Ed Harvey to steer clear of him. For Sutcliffe had a reputation for being sharp tongued, and what I saw of him in faculty meetings made me think him a colleague to respect from a distance. But, hearing from one of his former students that Sutcliffe would welcome some evening conversations, my friend Charles Rice and I invited him to have a beer. It was the first beer of many I drank in his company, for after our first evening together Sutcliffe and I became each other's habit. For me Sutcliffe was a well from which I could draw what I was still seeking to learn about American history, American literature, Kenyon College, Chalmers, the differences between American and English schools, and—the passion that bonded him to Chalmers—liberal education. Sutcliffe had thought more rigorously and more continuously about liberal education than any man before him, I could easily think. Teaching was his profession and his joy; he thought it the noblest of callings and he was never able to understand the growing scorn for teaching in the universities. He had a very great affection for his students and talked happily of them, even those on whom he expended gallons of red ink. He came to epitomize for me, as I believe he did for several generations of Kenyon undergraduates, what was best in the Chalmers Kenyon and what was most threatened as we drifted in the early Lund years. That he died at the age of fifty-one, in 1963, my first year as Dean, was the hardest blow I suffered in my professional life. The loss to his students and the College was not to be calculated.

Our conversations were shifted into a different framework in the summer of 1960, when he and I were two of the four-man team Kenyon was invited to send to Colorado College for a three-week session on undergraduate education, funded by the Carnegie Foundation. It was a remarkable time, for me the first opportunity I had ever had to organize my thinking about the purposes of undergraduate education, the first opportunity to compare Kenyon with other institutions. We found ourselves in the company of teams from about thirty other colleges and universities, some famous and some not known outside their home area. We of Kenyon paired with the team from Hampden-Sydney College, the only other all-male institution represented, and we found fruitful points of discussion with them. My strongest memory from those days has remained the opening plenary session, when the institutions were asked to have one of their team describe their college and its strengths. Sutcliffe spoke for us. After the round was completed and the coordinator asked for comments, Sutcliffe stood again. "I could not but note," he said, "that each of the small colleges represented here has claimed that a chief strength of the institution is that 'the students get to know the faculty.' Should we not ask, 'Are the faculty worth getting to know?'" The question was so characteristically Sutcliffe, the kind of question that had given him the reputation at Kenyon for having a sharp tongue, but he was surely right in saying that it is the question that must be answered.

Then there came another context for our conversations. Dean Bailey, increasingly alarmed at the demoralization of the faculty and Lund's failure to lead discussion of the College's future, urged the President to have the College engage in a self-study program over two years. It began in the fall of 1961. The program was directed in its first year by the faculty's most senior member, Paul Titus, Professor of Economics, and a steering committee composed of the five persons who would each chair a major committee. That committee soon brought before the faculty for its adoption a charge that would rule the study: that the faculty should seek to determine how Kenyon could become the best men's college in the country, *without reference to cost.* The italics are mine, the emphasis of one who spent thirty years as dean, provost, president learning that nearly every aspect of a college's life has somehow to be translated into a line item in a budget. But at the time it seemed to most of the faculty that our responsibility was to set the goal; it was the responsibility of the President and the trustees to provide the resources. Significantly, neither the business manager nor the development officer was invited to be part of the study.

Without the restraints that the realities of the College's situation should have provided, the first year became a sustained exercise in building castles in the air. Sutcliffe, chairing the committee on curriculum, chose me as a committee member. Others served on committees on instruction, on student life, on faculty, and on community relations. Remarkable as it seems now, there were no students on the committees that first year. There was much talk, much preparing and passing of position papers, much referring to what other colleges were doing. Virtually every suggestion, no matter at what remove from the facts of Kenyon's life, was entertained. Had somebody suggested that, with a chief problem being Kenyon's location in central Ohio, the College move to a more attractive and less competitive place, such as the Oregon coast, I am certain it would have been the topic of extended discussion. All of this went on while all members of the faculty, except Professor Titus, were still doing the ordinary amount of teaching, advising, and work on standing committees, so that we were all in a state of near exhaustion most of the time. Of an evening Sutcliffe and I compared our frustrations.

It was a very great surprise to me when Lund called me in and, explaining that Titus was going to take a year off to serve as a consultant to the Kingdom of Jordan, told me that he wished me to direct the self-study to its conclusion. I quickly voiced a dozen objections: I was at thirty-five still a very junior member of the faculty; I was too much involved in this and that.

To no avail. He held firm and, with the promise that a man would be hired for German so that I could have half-time off, I accepted reluctantly. When I accused Sutcliffe of having convinced Lund to appoint me, he denied it emphatically.

My first task was to get the chairmen of the committees to accept bounds for discussion, to identify targets, dates for reporting, a time to end it all. With that and my frequent sitting with the committees I got them to make headway. I brought students to the committees, and their presence helped give focus to some discussions. But even as we made progress, I became very concerned with the evidence of centrifugal forces operating in the faculty. I could see that some of my colleagues were approaching every question with an implicit question: how will this affect me and my department? With neither Lund nor Bailey offering any counter to that pull, such self-interest was threatening. I discussed it anxiously with Sutcliffe. It was more and more evident to us just how much the voice of Gordon Chalmers, reiterating his belief in required studies, in rigorous work on the central concerns of the College, his presence in all our formal discussions, had bonded the faculty into the effective body that it had been. With that center gone, it seemed to us, some new way of exerting a centripetal pull must be found.

The best and most lasting idea to come out of the self-study was one such way. It came, I believe, from the Dean of Students, certainly from the Committee on Student Life. I was captured by the idea and pushed hard for its adoption by the faculty. We created a body called the Campus Senate, which was to have authority over the non-academic aspects of student life and be an arena where students, faculty members, and administrators could discuss their concerns. The membership included the Dean of the College, the Dean of Students, the Registrar, four faculty members, the president and vice-president of the Student Council, and two or three more students elected at large. The President was a member *ex officio*, but it was not expected that he would be regularly in attendance. Meeting once a week for a couple of hours, the Campus Senate provided the centripetal pull we had hoped it would. Some of my best hours at Kenyon were spent on that committee, and there I came to know some of the best minds in the student body.

The crucial centripetal pull, Sutcliffe and I thought, must be in the curriculum, a power to which both faculty members and students would respond. That had been our central conviction in the many hours of discussion in his committee, but all too often any notion of center was lost in drawn-out arguments about the content of introductory courses, the hours of class meetings, the non-academic requirements for the degree. One thing I had learned from my time in Norton Hall was that freshmen were likely to see their introductory courses not as part of a planned program of general education, but as previews of major programs in the departments. I became ever more convinced that we needed to design a set of courses that would emphasize common experience for students and be effective introductions to what Chalmers thought were the essential studies. I imagined them being developed and taught by several members of the faculty together, with effort being made to show the complementing nature of the studies. I proposed five "basic courses," as I called them: language and literature (an expanded version of the existing freshman English course); history (Europe and America since 1776); science; philosophic and religious thought; the arts. The last was particularly controversial, for Chalmers, amateur painter of no mean skill that he was, seemed to have held the English conviction that the arts should not be in the academy, but have their own schools. Some of the faculty shared the view that, while young men might have a polite acquaintance with the arts, they should not take them so seriously as to want to work at them. I believed that the arts should be among the basic studies, though I was not then ready to argue that the departments should have major programs.

My great hope was that the basic courses would be so powerful that their content and the habits of mind learned in them would at least equal the importance of the student's major. I wanted faculty members to get their bearings from them and understand the need for constant integration of subject matters. The faculty debate was extensive and passionate; some of my newer colleagues felt threatened by the changes proposed. But a majority believed that the College urgently needed a fresh impetus, a restating of the principles that had guided it in its best years.

Hindsight tells me that we should have sought a massive grant from a foundation, which would have allowed several members of the faculty to take a year off to work out designs for the basic courses. Instead people worked at them over the summer and in their off hours. Nevertheless the courses were designed and taught, if not altogether in the form I had imagined them. In three instances I had to settle for subject matters being juxtaposed, rather than integrated, though I hoped for integration as time went on. They might all have succeeded, had it not been for the increasing power of departmentalism in the years that Kenyon underwent rapid expansion.

In another effort to stress the importance of keeping a subject in a context, I offered a new design for a student's major program. Instead of this being work in just the one department, I proposed that the program, accounting for ten of the seventeen units of credit required for graduation, be understood to be work in the major department and two cognate departments, the student's course of study being worked out with his advisor. That proposal was adopted much more readily than the basic courses had been.

And while I was knee deep in all of this in the fall and winter of 1962-63, my wife was pregnant with our first child, Margaret, who was born in April, even as we were moving into the final weeks of the self-study. I made a call on President Lund to tell him our joyful news and to bring him up to date on the progress of the committees. He congratulated me warmly and genuinely, with words about what his daughter, his only child, had meant to him. In that moment I was truly fond of him. Though by then nearly despised across the College, Lund was a warm and friendly man, quick to offer a hand or lend sympathy. Sutcliffe, spending hours with him in pursuit of rabbits, had always enjoyed the man Lund was, if not the president he was. As I had come to know him better in the months I had been reporting to him regularly, I had come increasingly to feel sorry for him, called on, as he had been, to meet expectations that Chalmers himself could not have met. It was as unhappy a thing for him as it was for us that the trustees had put a square peg into a round hole.

As I was rising to leave, Lund bade me remain seated. There was something else he wanted to talk to me about. Frank Bailey, he said, wished to retire at the end of June; Lund had decided I should become Dean. I was stunned. There had been no rumor of Bailey's wishing to retire, though he had informed Lund of his wishes months before; had I known of it, I should not have wished to be a candidate to succeed him. I protested. I was happy being the professor that I was. I had just become chief reader for the Advanced Placement Program in German. I pleaded with him not to ask that of me. Surely, I said, Sutcliffe was the one who ought to be his choice. He respected no man more than Sutcliffe, Lund rejoined, but his obviously declining health ruled him out. The position demanded energies Sutcliffe no longer had. He was emphatic that I was the one he intended to appoint. He allowed that I should "sleep on it" and talk it over with my wife, but, he emphasized in ending our conversation, I was to tell nobody else. I disobeyed him and talked it over with Sutcliffe that very evening. He was as emphatic as Lund had been that I should take the position. With the self-study coming to a fairly successful conclusion, the faculty would have confidence in me, he said. He promised his help. Who else if not you? he asked.

Gretchen was not happy to hear of my conversation with Lund. She knew enough about Kenyon matters to fear that the pressures on me would be destructive. I had very great doubts myself about my ability to succeed in the position, but Sutcliffe's "If not you, who else?" had made me think hard about becoming Dean. A second talk with Sutcliffe and a discussion with Aldrich, who said that he—and others, he was certain—would give me strong support convinced me to tell the President I would do it.

Lund granted Bailey's wish that he be allowed to name me publicly as his successor. The morning after the announcement I was visited in my office by the College's business manager, Sam Lord, a man I barely knew, he having come to the College only in the previous year. He offered his congratulations and at once went on to say, "You can do one of two things now. You can either use this appointment as a stepping stone to a better job or you can stay here and try to make Kenyon into a decent college once again." I hastened to say that I fully intended to remain as Dean. He said, obviously pleased by my reply, "Then the first thing you should know is that Kenyon has a million dollars of unpaid bills."

Chapter VI
Salvation in Old Ideas

Sam Lord became my closest colleague. In a thankless job, the business manager of a desperately struggling college, he was often called the "abominable No-man," so frequently did he have to deny requests. He introduced a notion brand-new to Kenyon: achieve a balanced budget, something that I can believe Kenyon had never before known in its troubled financial history. With the enthusiastic backing of the trustees, Lord preached the importance of the College's not spending more than it took in, but it was not until 1968 that we managed to realize that goal for the first time. Kenyon has done it ever since. Before we reached that happy state, Sam and I had some very anxious years together.

After Sam shocked me with his first revelation of Kenyon's awful predicament—debts that would be the equivalent of ten million dollars in 2004—I resolved to know more about the College's financial situation. In these times, when colleges routinely publish financial statements and the salary of the president is advertised in the student newspaper, it will seem strange to some to learn that this was not always the case. Indeed, for the greater part of the past century information about an institution's finances was kept under wraps. In the year I became Dean of the College the only knowledge of the operating budget the faculty had was the average salary paid to faculty members. Studying the budget, when I got my hands on it after July 1, was a continuing shock. Only when I was done was it clear to me just how close to bankruptcy Kenyon was. It was not the last time I was to wonder whether I had bitten off more than I could chew.

I feared that, if this information were made known to the faculty, there would be an exodus of disastrous proportions. It seemed prudent to keep it all to myself; the faculty's salary figures were enough to tell them that there was little financial health in Gambier.

From Lord I had quickly gathered that the President showed little concern about the College's financial problems. Lund seemed to believe that Kenyon could survive until his retirement; he seemed unconcerned about what came after. I decided to leave to Lord any conversations with Lund about budget matters, limiting my early talks with him to immediate academic problems. He listened attentively, but unresponsively. I was to understand, his attitude said, that those were my problems, not his.

In my first few days in office I called on the other members of the President's staff, quickly learning from them that they would welcome greater contact with me than they had had with my predecessor. It was a great surprise to me to learn that the President met with his people only individually and then irregularly; there were no staff meetings. The right hand of the staff didn't know what the left was doing. I at once put it to Lund that we who reported to him would welcome having joint meetings with him, a proposal that annoyed him. He didn't believe in staff meetings, he said, they simply wasted time. However, he added at once, if I wished to have regular meetings with the others, I was welcome to do so.

I invited my new colleagues to join me in my office at nine the following Monday morning. That would become a weekly feature for the remainder of Lund's term in office. We were easily accommodated in my office, for the "administration"—it seems almost comic to call us that—was a very small body. Besides me, those who reported to the President were the Dean of Students, the business manager, the director of admissions, the director of development, and the chaplain. To that number, with the agreement of the others, I added the registrar, whom I had chosen for the position after knowing him for a few years as assistant director of admissions. I already had in mind having a registrar who could do institutional research.

We began with each of us giving an assessment of what he thought to be the chief problem in his office. For nearly everybody, the first issue was the President's indifference. It was very clear that we were a ship without a captain. Beside that, there came from every quarter distressingly negative reports on the College's circumstances. Kenyon ranked far below colleges of its kind in alumni support; the admissions office was finding it ever more difficult to attract strong students; morale everywhere was low. Kenyon's endowment was one-tenth the size of the Williams College endowment. But it was Lord's report, of course, which sounded increasingly like a death knell. Kenyon was continuing to live beyond its means, as meagerly as we were living. Some solution had to be found quickly and, in Sam's view, the only answer was more predictable income from a larger student body. We could not, after Lund's rejection of Ford, hope for any foundation help, but Sam had already established that the federal government was offering loans and even grants to private colleges that were proposing significant growth.

It was Lord who introduced the rest of us to the work of a Ford Foundation economist, Sydney Tickton, the man believed to have excited Ford's interest in the problems of private colleges. Tickton's analysis of their problems was a simple one: the costs of operation were rising; there was deferred maintenance everywhere;

changes in the tax laws made it likely that colleges would find it difficult to increase trustee and alumni giving. His solution: increasing enrollments without proportionate increases in staffing would spread the costs of overhead and allow for additional spending. Tickton's persuasive arguments, Lord's analyses, and echoes of faculty voices in the self-study combined to bring me quickly to the belief that we must plan a larger Kenyon College. I was not slow to damn Lund for having so cavalierly rejected the interest of the Ford Foundation. We had let slip an opportunity that could not be recaptured.

My colleagues were ready to see the soundness of the Tickton answer, but against that was the dismal report from the admissions director. He thought it impossible for Kenyon to double its enrollment, even with further lowering of admissions requirements. There was a lot of sad shaking of heads, anxious looks, body language that spoke defeat. But then somebody—was it I? I no longer know for certain—proposed that we admit women.

It is not easy now, with nearly all the once all-male institutions having later come to our conclusions, to remember what an utterly shocking idea that was for us to sound. Kingman Brewster, President of Yale, was then still three years away from making his declaration that women would "never darken the door of Yale University," words he was to eat not long after. Amherst, Haverford, and Williams seemed supremely confident of an all-male future for themselves. We had heard no whispers of any other men's college contemplating this drastic step.

The only alumnus in our number that day, the director of development, said at once that the alumni would never stand for coeducation in Gambier. Neither would the trustees agree, others said. It was hard for me to challenge that, since I knew that Kenyon men almost invariably associated with its all-male character those things they cherished most about the College.

Setting aside the alumni and trustees for the moment, though I knew they would have to be reckoned with, I argued what seemed to me the obvious advantages of having women in the College. Not least was that it seemed to me that women would raise the tone of the College; the behavior of some of our students seemed lately to have approached the barbaric. But most of all it seemed to me that we could make a powerful case for believing that it would not be difficult to attract very able women to the College and that that, in turn, would improve our ability to attract good male candidates. There seemed to me, persuaded as I was by Sydney Tickton's arguments, no real alternative for Kenyon.

Salvation in Old Ideas

Perhaps it was because we had all come to recognize just how serious our situation was that those in my office that day found the straw of a coeducational Kenyon not impossible to grasp. From that point forward it was central to our discussions and the more the responses to the idea bounced back and forth across the room, the more wedded to it I became. Surely, if our argument were sound, the trustees and the alumni could be persuaded.

Because I was so concerned about the low morale in the faculty, I was eager to put before them the fruits of our staff discussions. I had to give them hope that the College could look to a future. Accordingly I had a meeting with the chairs of departments and, after giving them information about the budget, the recruitment of students, and alumni giving, I set out the case for a larger and coeducational Kenyon. There were at once some smiles in the room and voices of support. But there were doubters. Inevitably there were those who feared the alumni would persuade the trustees not to give the idea a serious hearing.

I think it was that very evening when I came to believe that we could persuade the alumni and eventually the trustees by proposing a model I had lived with for three years at Harvard. Women students in my courses there were not officially Harvard students; they were members of Radcliffe College, a coordinate institution with its own campus and administration, but without a faculty. Surely that same way of organizing would work for us. The idea was well received by my staff colleagues the following Monday morning; the development officer even imagined a significant major gift to put a family name on the coordinate college. Our optimism and our enthusiasm grew.

Though Lund was neither optimistic nor enthusiastic—we didn't expect it—he was yet willing to see us move ahead to model building. Lord would look at the financial aspects of the imagined solution, while I would work at staffing and curriculum questions. To that end I undertook to put questions to twenty-five colleges, some women's colleges, some co-ed. I needed to know how women distributed themselves across departments, what services colleges provided them, what additional support staff we would need. Armed with that information I convened the chairs again and asked them to think of what staffs their department would need for the student bodies we were imagining. Within the span of two academic years we had completed a plan that could be put before the trustees.

While this planning and the attendant discussions were at the center of my activity, I had many other irons in my fire. Most happily, we were parents again. Our younger daughter, Elizabeth, was born in 1966. I continued to teach one course each semester; I had become a member of the selection committee for Michigan and Ohio of the Woodrow Wilson Fellowship program; I was trying to learn what our involvement was in the Great Lakes Colleges Association, a consortium of a dozen colleges, in Ohio (six), Indiana and Michigan (three each). But I was also having to face what I had dreaded: resignations from the faculty. There was no great number, but in a faculty of some forty people even a couple made a great difference. And in the second year of my tenure *both* members of political science resigned, one to leave the profession altogether, the other to go as chairman to the department at UCLA. It was a devastating blow—both men were highly regarded professors—and it was felt across the faculty and the student body. But, remarkably, their departure opened the door to one of the happiest features of my seventeen years as Dean and Provost.

The chairman of the Woodrow Wilson committee, Dean of the Honors Council at the University of Michigan, responded to my appeal for help by putting me in touch with the only political philosopher in a department of behaviorists. Robert Horwitz was not happy in that company. He was a graduate of Amherst College who, after serving in the U.S. Army during WWII, had earned a doctorate in a redoubtable department at the University of Chicago. He agreed to visit Kenyon and the two of us were friends and colleagues immediately.

Horwitz was to demonstrate compellingly what a visionary chairman can do for an academic department. The faculty members he recruited over the next several years gave the department such strength that it was the only undergraduate department of political science mentioned in the same breath as the powerhouse departments at the University of Toronto, Chicago, and Cornell. Within a few years he had lured to Kenyon a public affairs program that had graced the University of Chicago for some years, and that in turn brought some very distinguished thinkers to Gambier for conferences. Those sessions were as significant for Kenyon's name and morale as the conferences Chalmers had put on in the 'fifties. I was often to report to Kenyon's alumni in later years that Horwitz had created a department which, in its teaching, scholarship, and national reputation, could rival the College's celebrated Department of English. No less a joy to me was the fact that Horwitz and his colleagues were champions of liberal education and made teaching their first priority.

I had some difficulty reconciling myself to the GLCA consortium and its purposes. It had come into being the year before I became Dean, modeling itself on the four-year-old consortium of like size, the Associated Colleges of the Midwest. Those institutions, in Illinois, Iowa, Wisconsin, and Minnesota, had banded together out of a common interest in creating overseas programs. It was quite easy in the 'sixties, when European salaries and operational costs were very low, to run such programs at little cost and have small numbers of students with legitimate interests spend terms in France, Spain, and Germany. Some colleges in the GLCA which already had their own modest programs thought to expand them. Indeed, the proposed consortium programs adopted before I became Dean already imagined much larger groups of students spending a semester or even a year abroad. I had urged my colleagues to oppose the plan. I was not sympathetic to the idea of students going to a country to study when they had no adequate knowledge of its language, to say nothing of its culture. After the years I had spent seeking to understand things German, I was offended by the notion that a term in Germany was going to have students returning with an understanding in depth. The superficial seemed to me far more dangerous in the end than confessed ignorance. I rejected, too, the notion that a semester abroad, spent largely in sightseeing and casual learning, was the "equivalent" of a semester at the College. Going to the zoo, I argued, was not the same as studying natural history. I was all for having students study abroad after four years at Kenyon; we had Fulbright winners who had proved the worth of that. But I was on the losing side. By a very large majority my colleagues supported the President, telling me that, after all, it would be a very small number of Kenyon students who would wish to take advantage of such an opportunity. None of them could have possibly foreseen a time when students would think it a "right" that they have a semester in exotic places, getting full academic credit for it; none of them could have understood what a drain on our resources it would be when dozens of students decided to absent themselves for a semester or a year to go to a GLCA program. In all too short a time we were being asked by the GLCA office to *recruit* students to support the overseas programs, and we were hosts to representatives of those programs who came to Gambier straightforwardly to recruit. Beneath all of my resistance to such recruiting, of course, lay the anxious belief that the programs of the consortium, growing in number and magnetic power, were yet more threats to the idea of the residential liberal arts college I was struggling to preserve. I had very real fears that, in accepting an "equivalent" for a Kenyon semester, we should be destroying the integrity of the degree.

The cheapening of the degree became a matter of even greater concern to me in later years, as my faculty colleagues, concerned about rising costs for students, became willing to recognize work at other institutions as being the "equivalent" of Kenyon work. First it was transfer credit from the academic year of any accredited institution, liberal arts college or no; then it was credit for work in summer schools. I recall being visited in the late 'seventies by a bright young woman who first told me that she was going to be graduating from the College after only two and a half years. She had been granted a half year's credit for Advanced Placement courses taken in high school and had then racked up credits in summer school at a community college. She described the courses as "a joke." But she had come to my office to fault me for letting her get away with a "cheap degree." Her faculty advisers had approved her summer school registrations in advance, because she wanted to accelerate and get on to law school. Hers was the worst case I knew of, but there were far too many early graduations for my comfort. I feared for our traditions.

That we would, in fact, seek to preserve in the larger Kenyon the best of the Chalmers legacy was the first assurance I had given my faculty colleagues, and it was the assurance I would eventually give to the College's trustees and the alumni groups I addressed. I told them we wished above all to preserve what we saw as the essential identity of Kenyon College: a small, intimate, residential college of the liberal arts staffed by highly competent and accessible teacher/scholars. As we advanced with our plans for change, I was certain we could say confidently that we could be true to those pledges.

It was, in fact, with the firm belief that some change would not only preserve, but strengthen, the College's purposes that I went before the faculty in 1966 to propose that the arts departments, together with the Department of Religion, should be allowed to offer major programs. They knew my convictions about the appropriate place of the arts in the liberal curriculum; now I argued that the time had come for the departments in question to have full status in the College. They had so long existed on the periphery that it was difficult for some of my colleagues to accept the notion. The cause of the arts had been considerably advanced with the addition to the faculty of Joseph Slate, a former newspaperman who had earned an M.F.A. in studio art at Yale. Personable and eloquent, Slate did much to persuade his colleagues when I did not. He was to build Art into one of Kenyon's best departments. The motion passed, with Religion becoming Religious Studies and, eventually, a force to be reckoned with in the humanities division. (Today that department has seven full-time faculty members, while Philosophy, for so many years a power in the humanities, has four.)

Inevitably, in the discussion about majors in the arts, questions were raised about future facilities needs and staffing for the departments. I was able to assure my colleagues that our plans for the larger College included appropriate facilities and that more faculty would be added as enrollments grew. That the faculty readily accepted those arguments was evidence that, by 1966, the idea of the larger, coeducational Kenyon was driving the institution's thinking and, like a snowball rolling downhill, it was gathering momentum and mass in the form of optimistic thinking about the future. It was that idea which kept at the College a number of people who could and likely would have departed, had not that notion been early released to the faculty.

Still, there were those for whom President Lund remained such a question mark that they found it difficult to believe that things would happen as I was saying they would. Time and again individual members came to my office to confess their anxiety and seek reassurance. I spent a lot of time on pep talks, and more and more of my time in committees was spent in elaborating on what I believed would come to pass. But an underlying suspicion remained, sometimes joining all of us in the senior staff to Lund.

It came to the surface in an indirect fashion. It was in 1966, as I recall, that a younger colleague came to my office, representing a committee that was undertaking, under the leadership of Professor Finkbeiner, an evaluation of standing committees and the faculty's role in them. He inquired about some history he, a recent addition to the faculty, didn't know. He asked about my sense of what each committee did and how effectively it did it. I heard nothing more about the committee's activity until one day Professor Finkbeiner called on me to show me the reorganization of the committees he planned to offer the faculty. Most apparent to me was that the Dean of the College was no longer chair of any standing committee, whereas I, following Bailey's example, had chaired three or four of them. I had always seen that as a way of relieving members of the faculty of busy work, but Finkbeiner, arguing for the faculty's greater involvement in the business side of the institution, said that "after all, these are faculty committees." I was at once struck by the portent of his statement. Until that moment I had used the word "faculty" in such matters interchangeably with "College." The committees had seemed to me clearly to exist to do the work of the College; they were a prime way of having members of the faculty involved in important aspects, such as admissions and student life, of the institution's life. I had never thought of myself, becoming Dean, as having left the faculty. I remained a teaching member of the department; I continued to think of myself as a professor of German, temporarily performing another function in the College. It was a shock to understand that I was not seen as I saw myself. It was my first brief encounter with the sense of "them and us," administration and faculty as coexisting but separate bodies, which would become ever more prominent in the life of colleges and which would certainly alter the character of Kenyon College. But, taken aback, I raised no objection then and the wisdom of hindsight tells me that I ought to have done so.

(That wonderful way of characterizing people as "members of the College," which Gordon Chalmers used for students, faculty members, and staff members alike, has disappeared in a time when there is a seemingly unbridgeable gap, even in some small colleges, between the faculty and the administration. On some campuses there is crackling hostility between the two bodies, on many others a faculty suspicion of the administration that approaches paranoia. Some years ago I appointed a member of the faculty, well liked and respected by his colleagues, to be associate dean. He resigned the position after his first year in office, unable to endure the sudden rejection he found in the words of a faculty member who, accosting him on the parking lot, said, "I never thought you would betray your colleagues.")

In the spring and fall issues of the *Alumni Bulletin* of 1965, Sam Lord and I made our respective arguments for our plan to Kenyon's graduates and friends, Lord arguing the need for change, I arguing the proposed solution. Suddenly I began to get a lot of mail. There were one or two letters of support, but the overwhelming number were hostile. I was invited to leave. I was even threatened. I was urged to be honest about my wish to see women at Kenyon, which those writers knew for certain was a none too subtle way of making Kenyon as dry a campus as Denison or Oberlin. Clearly, many alumni felt betrayed. Whereas we had argued from the outset that our solution to Kenyon's crisis was to put women into Kenyon classrooms with Kenyon faculty members, they had interpreted talk of a "coordinate college for women" to mean the creation of a completely separate, autonomous institution. Disappointed as I was by the overwhelmingly negative response to our arguments, I nonetheless understood the anxieties of my critics. They feared that Kenyon's character would be lost. They were not persuaded by the Harvard-Radcliffe solution I had proposed; women would be in Gambier and that, as they saw it, would change everything. (Years later I had other letters from some of those alumni, expressing apology and regret: their daughters were happily enrolled at Kenyon.)

Nothing had concerned me more over the two years of our inquiries and reflections than preserving the essential character of Kenyon College. I had read enough pieces in the professional literature arguing that the greatest mistake a college could make was in changing its established character, and everything I had come to value in my professional life was contained within the idea of the Chalmers Kenyon. Throughout I had argued that the essential college was not finally shaped by the gender of the student body. I was confident in my belief that young women should have the same liberal education in the same studies as young men. I could not accept the argument offered by some that women *students* were different; my experience argued the opposite. I continued to believe that the essential college should have both men and women members. Among the faculty that view had won the day, but not among the undergraduates. As late as the spring of 1969, just a few months before the first women were to arrive, the College newspaper reported that 82% of the students were "unalterably opposed" to the coming of women. Nevertheless we persisted in our belief that our plan was the only solution to Kenyon's overwhelming financial problems. We had convinced a majority of the trustees, and most importantly the chairman of the board, of the rightness of our thinking, and we had their permission to develop a full-scale proposal for their consideration, though with no commitment to action. It was a truly exciting time and I was filled with high optimism about the College's future.

While debate raged on, President Lund continued to be a detached, but not unfriendly, observer. He was content to have us work at our plans without input from him.

With Sam Lord having convincing evidence that the College could float a bond issue through the State of Ohio to finance most of the new construction and with the promise of federal grants and loans, the trustees permitted us to engage architects to produce plans. We interviewed a half dozen firms, asking them to sketch a solution to the problem we gave them: how to house, provide dining facilities, laundry, and recreational lounges for 650 women. Importantly, too, we asked them to propose where these should be sited so as to have the women students have ready access to classrooms. One imaginative architect offered us a twenty-some storied building to house all we needed, to be built in the lovely open space at the heart of the College Park. He had never visited Gambier, being content to work from the map of the College and the village that had been supplied him. I hope we managed to keep a straight face so long as he was in the room.

In October 1967, the trustees announced a campaign to raise many millions of dollars, much of it to be used for the construction of a new residential campus and facilities for the arts and sciences. My colleagues and I were jubilant. We had been persuasive and we had the blueprint of a program that would guarantee Kenyon's future life. I spent the happiest Sunday I had known in a very long time.

Just before nine on Monday morning President Lund entered my office through a side door not ordinarily used by visitors. His face was grim. He sat down in a chair beside the door and, without prelude, announced, "I am not going to let it happen." I did not know at that moment, startled as I was to see Lund in the building at that time of day, what the antecedent of "it" was.

He didn't leave me in the dark. He said in a voice trembling with passion that he had gone along with all the talk and planning, always believing that in the end the powerful opponents of our plan on the board would ensure its rejection. In particular he had relied on the board's overwhelmingly wealthiest member, a Harvard graduate who had been first to rise to speak against the proposal when I first put it before the board. That trustee had declared that women would "destroy Kenyon, just as they have Harvard." But George Gund had failed to dissuade his fellow trustees, thus destroying Lund's last hope.

Lund continued: he had his own plans, carefully worked out, for his final few years before retirement and they did not include heading a fundraising drive. He acknowledged that the plan we had presented was indeed what Kenyon should do, but not in his tenure. "After I'm gone," he said, "you can become president and put your plan in place." With that he left. I recall having said not a word in reply.

A moment later my secretary opened my office door and admitted my staff colleagues. Within a minute their faces were as long as mine. Despairing, we adjourned. After a time I left the building and went home to my wife and daughters, desperately needing comfort.

Salvation in Old Ideas

I returned to my office that afternoon, having already cancelled appointments. I sat, seeking to take hold of the full import of Lund's declaration. My only conclusion was that Kenyon would now suffer a lingering death, stretched over perhaps four or five years. And my career was in shambles, for I had staked everything on that one idea.

At about three that afternoon my secretary told me that a good friend of mine was on the phone. He said that his university, one of the best in the Middle West, was looking for a dean of its undergraduate division and he thought me the perfect candidate for the job, for their president, concerned about the brightest and best in the undergraduate body, was thinking of creating a residential college within the university's structure. Would I come for interview? Hardly believing that I was being thrown a lifeline, I told him that, if he had called at any time before that day, I would have politely declined. But now, yes, I would come.

On Thursday morning early the Vice President for Academic Affairs phoned to offer me the position and asked me to respond to his offer no later than Saturday morning. After further conversation with my wife, I wrote a letter resigning my Kenyon position and dropped it off at the President's residence on my way to my office. (I had earlier informed him that I was going for an interview and he had not seemed surprised.) Evidently thinking that it was only the larger salary that would cause me to leave Kenyon, he asked only that I not respond to the offer until he had talked to the chairman of the board. Just minutes later the chairman himself called me. He, a man I greatly respected, asked me to promise that I would take no action until he had had a face to face talk with me. He promised to be in Gambier the next morning. Before he returned to Louisville he had interviewed members of the staff and faculty and had secured Lund's resignation, to come at the end of the academic year. He urged me not to leave, saying "Kenyon needs you." I promised him I would stay and I informed the university that, having put my hand to the Kenyon plough, I had to complete the furrow.

Lund held no grudges. He at once made a courageous appearance before the faculty, announcing his resignation, and he held his head high for his remaining months at Kenyon. Nobody was sorry to see him go, but those who knew his decent human instincts were sorry for him. He had been put into an office he had never fitted.

Chapter VII
The Magic Mountain

It was widely assumed that I would follow Lund into office. A colleague, who had watched Lund turn to shake hands with me after announcing his resignation to the assembled faculty, told me that he thought he was "seeing the passing of the torch." But I had already told the chairman of the board that I had no wish to be President, partly because, given the College's immediate circumstances and the years of construction and financing that lay ahead of us, the need was for a manager and fund raiser. In neither of those roles did I see myself. I thought the best thing I could do was to try to provide the academic leadership Kenyon would need in a time of change. Just how much change would be thrust upon us in the next few years I could not possibly have foreseen.

But my staff colleagues and I were very conscious of the need for somebody immediately to occupy the office Lund would vacate at the end of June. The College could not stand a year of searching for a successor while I served as interim president. The talk in my office on the Monday morning was all of the need to move on, without a moment's delay, with the plan that would save Kenyon from disaster.

I put forward the name of William G. Caples, loyal alumnus, trustee, lawyer, vice-

The Essential College

president of Inland Steel, long-serving member and sometime chairman of the Chicago School Board. There was an immediate nodding of heads and vocal agreement. Caples had supported our plans from the beginning, and his larger support of education was well known. We readily imagined that he could be a successful fund raiser.

Caples, startled by the proposal, as the chairman of the board had been, thought the faculty would not accept a non-academic in the office, but I counted on the faculty's recognizing the need for immediate leadership. They had been grateful, besides, for Caples's successful negotiation of the seminary's separation and they knew of his strong support for the plan for change. When the chairman was later able to tell him that the poll he requested showed the faculty virtually unanimous in supporting the idea, he accepted. In April 1968 his appointment was made known. He declared himself willing to serve a six-year term, long enough to see the changes accomplished. He made a very great financial sacrifice in taking on the position and, even before he took office, he began to press forward with the plans for the coordinate college. In his first years Caples provided the strong leadership and direction we needed.

The program went forward smoothly over the next three years. A new residential campus came into being, as close to classrooms as were the freshmen men's dormitories. Everybody agreed that the new architecture was a great success and the siting of the buildings a particularly pleasing blending into the landscape.

Those remarkable young women who entered in September 1969, all except one being first-year students, secured the success of the entire venture. They bravely entered classrooms and labs where no woman had ever trod, suffered some outrageous behavior from the few hold-outs among the upperclassmen, and endured occasional condescension from faculty members. In her second year one of those women came to my office, eyes flashing. She had just come from the science department where she was to major; the chairman, surprised greatly by her declaration, had remarked, "Oh, I had always thought of mine as a man's subject." He wasn't the only one who lived and learned. But what those women and their successors proved beyond a doubt was that their presence did not in any way alter the academic life of Kenyon College, except to improve it. I am grateful to all of them for saving Kenyon.

Two years after the first women arrived, the trustees abandoned the "coordinate" notion and made Kenyon College wholly coeducational. It was what the women wished. They had come to Gambier believing that they would be Kenyon's students; to be "coordinate" made no sense to them. Neither, once they were with us, did it seem sensible to us. "Coordinate" had been a psychological bridge that allowed us to cross over into a new existence.

While we quickly grew used to the presence of women, the drastically larger student and faculty bodies brought changes we were less quick to recognize. With all the gains we made, there were some losses. Professor Baker, a contemporary of mine in the College, called by my office to say emphatically, "We should have stopped at eight hundred. We don't know one another any more." By that time the student body was nearly twice that size and, as Bob Baker meant, we had faculty colleagues whom we barely recognized when we met them on Middle Path. Classes were larger than they had been, though having twelve students in a class rather than eight didn't really alter it. Still, faculty members sensed that they were slower to know their students and there was a feeling, if only temporarily, that Gambier had suddenly become a little crowded. It was the inevitable consequence of our having so quickly expanded; colleges which spread their growth over several years, as nearly all did, were more comfortable with their changes, though any college that doubled its size had to adjust to different expectations. We didn't do enough to compensate for the loss of easy familiarity and quick socialization. Caples proved in those first years to be an excellent manager. He believed firmly in staff meetings and staff responsibilities. He expected hard work; he worked hard himself, a refreshing and invigorating change for the College. As I think back on his first couple of years in office, I believe that we could not have had a better leader for the time and circumstances, particularly in the crisis year of 1970, the year of Kent State.

We had been moving towards that climactic moment for some time. The Civil Rights Movement, the assassinations of the Kennedy brothers and of Martin Luther King, and above all the anti-Vietnam War protests had brought anger to America's campuses such as we had never seen before. Gambier had been relatively quiet. Perhaps the ongoing drama of the preparations for the first women students occupied us to the degree that the larger world's tumult did not touch us as much as it might have done. But the major factor, I am convinced, was that students knew of faculty members' sympathies to their concerns and protests; they knew their voices were heard and respected. The large majority of students did not approve of the few who painted slogans on the walls of Chalmers Library one weekend. There was a style to protest at Kenyon; protest could find appropriate channels: the newspaper, the faculty office, student council meetings, the Campus Senate. Until 1970 I had no sense that the rage in the country would threaten the College and its work. But Kent State was different.

For one thing, it was so very close. Kent is less than two hours by car from Gambier. There was a strong sense that those killed were our people. They seemed the victims of an unfeeling, unresponsive system. Detached discussion of this event would not be enough.

Rosse Hall, the College's auditorium, was packed with people from the village as well as students, faculty, and staff members, one evening after another. There were provocateurs from Ohio State who took the platform. The call, again and again, was that the College should be closed down, in solidarity with those campuses that had already declared a shutdown. But at Kenyon we saw a triumph of liberal education. Our students had been educated to the belief that, no matter how strongly one holds one's views, there are other voices to be heard. The most persuasive voice in Rosse Hall on the final evening proved to be that of a Jewish refugee from Hitler's universities. Eugen Kullman, professor of religious studies, spoke quietly of the European tyrants who had sought to stifle dissent by shutting down schools and universities. Kenyon, he said, was not the voice of institutionalized tyranny; it was a place where people had gathered to teach and learn—together. He urged that Kenyon set a better example and stay open, doing its work.

I was never so proud to be a member of Kenyon College as I was in the time that followed that tumultuous evening. The students trusted their teachers; the professors trusted the students. And all admired President Caples's efforts to organize fellow presidents to seek a meeting with the governor of Ohio. The faculty, in a special meeting, broke precedent and invited two student leaders to join them in discussing how we might best go forward. It was agreed that classes should continue, that examinations be held, that there should be a few days of special seminars on issues, and that Commencement should take place as scheduled. In another precedent the faculty agreed that seniors who were too upset to attend Commencement exercises and graduate with their class could receive their degree *in absentia*. I believe there were just two students who took advantage of that. Kenyon was the only college in Ohio that completed its scheduled work and held graduation exercises.

The 'sixties and 'seventies inflicted more damage on liberal education and liberal arts colleges than had been seen in any other time in our history. The slogans of the day, "Do your own thing" and "If it feels good, do it," challenged every tenet of liberal education. Not only were students urged to trust nobody over thirty, they were simultaneously invited to trust no idea over thirty, no institutional form with a history. Virtually every form, in fact, except the improvisation of the moment, was suspect. To destroy the building was to destroy the idea contained within it. To occupy the president's office, which was the most popular tactic of campus revolutionaries, was to stop the institution from doing its work altogether. Colleges and universities were depicted by radicals as instruments of repression and capitalism; they stood in the way of the revolution. The very idea of a college was often ridiculed; better to have a continuing demonstration which could embrace whatever object of scorn the leaders set up. We commonly talk of the "student revolution" of those decades, but the gurus of the movement and often its campus leaders were dissident faculty members—and sometimes presidents and deans.

The most radical transformation of a liberal arts college I witnessed was at an Ohio and GLCA neighbor. Those of us who served on the Woodrow Wilson Fellowship Committee had held that college in high esteem, for its seniors were among the very best candidates we saw. I knew some very fine faculty members there, nearly all of whom eventually left after a new president and dean undertook to turn the college into "a vehicle for social change." Nowhere else did traditional practice get shorter shrift. Within a remarkably short span of time the faculty abandoned grades and conventional courses. An experimental freshman year emphasized experiential learning, while promotion to the sophomore class required only that a freshman have had a "meaningful experience." A female student was granted academic credit for time spent in a Cincinnati jail, where she had been sentenced for her part in a violent demonstration. She was said to be getting there the "equivalent" of a semester on campus. The last time I visited the college, for a GLCA deans' meeting in the middle 'seventies, there were barbed wire barricades across a town street that runs through the campus, painted slogans covering every building, and signs that declared that the revolution had come to Ohio.

Those who led that college believed that they were creating a new model of the American college, with branch storefront operations in other places, even faraway California. These were to be the instruments of radical political and social change, but they were largely fueled by hostility to the Vietnam War and, with its end, revolutionary zeal seemed to evaporate rather quickly.

At many other colleges and universities there were similar assaults on traditional form. Eliminating grades and creating coed dorms were the most common agenda items. But running a close third was the dismantling of the structured curriculum. In the radicals' vocabulary a required course was a form of tyranny. Courses on anything but contemporary topics were branded as irrelevant. Many church-related colleges, fearful of being thought over thirty, hastily severed ties with their denominations. Any suggestion of formal attire was suspect, some faculty joining the students in the rush to don jeans and t-shirts, once the clothing of the underprivileged. In many colleges students were allowed to cross the platform at Commencement dressed in any way they wished. (Like many other academic traditions, Commencement exercises have been permanently changed; the solemnity of academic regalia worn by the faculty is more than balanced now by the hoots and hollers from the students and their families.) And, of course, civil discourse was seen as the means by which the powerful suppressed the weak, so crudity was in its stead introduced into the classroom and the faculty meeting. The new way for faculty members to shock their bourgeois students out of their smug conventional thinking was to pepper their lectures with those words George Carlin said couldn't be used on television.

Students did not, of course, ever control the form of the curriculum or the requirements for the degree. They may have voiced their discontents, sought to bring pressure, demonstrated outside a faculty meeting or two, but the authority over the curriculum remained in the hands of the faculty. In many an institution virtually nothing remained of the traditional curriculum by the mid-seventies. The President of Amherst College, viewing what his faculty had wrought, is reported to have said that the College would seem to be saying to its freshmen come September, "This semester the College will offer two hundred and some courses; take any four." College after college adopted the remarkable belief that eighteen-year-olds were better able to create a course of study for themselves than their professors were. Students in many colleges were turned loose to "do their own thing," freed from distribution or general education requirements, able if they wished to spend most of their time playing their strengths. At Wesleyan of Connecticut a student was granted a B.A. degree after having taken only one course outside the Department of Mathematics. Elsewhere students moved into premature specialization with a vengeance, the forms and substance of liberal education discarded.

But a far more lasting menace came to Kenyon, as it did to every other college, when drug use became a common phenomenon. We had always had students who drank too much, students who got speeding tickets, students who bounced a check or two. Now, for the first time, we had to recognize that we had students who were regularly and consciously breaking the law, using LSD and other drugs; even worse we had a few who were selling drugs to their fellows. Though President Caples delivered an impassioned speech on the Chalmers Library steps, warning students that the College could not tolerate abuse of the law, we were in fact helpless to do much about drug users. We could and did offer seminars, we could speak to the dangers, set rules, but in the end we faced the awesome fact that some of our undergraduates were willing to ingest or inject substances, the nature of which they did not know. In the late 'seventies I was visited by a '64 graduate, who was back for the first time since he graduated. I asked him what change had struck him most. Without a second's pause he said, "The closed doors in the dorms." In his day, he said, people kept their doors open, always available to visitors; now they didn't want to be caught smoking pot. Such withdrawal obviously posed a threat to an institution which thought constant interaction among its members a crucial component of liberal education. Some faculty members acknowledged to me that they found themselves viewing students with suspicion; others were certain that the quality of student work had fallen off. Inevitably, as the years went on, we were to wonder about one or two of our colleagues. Drug use, ego gratification in the *nth* degree, is a virulent force working against all that liberal education has embodied. The "drug culture," as it has come pathetically to be called, has affected all of education, from its lowest to its highest levels, and one must wonder whether we shall ever recover from its effects. Colleges seem to have decided that living with drugs is like living with student cars on campus, an accommodation to the new realities in higher education.

The lifting of constraints in the 'seventies accounts too, I must think, for the later emergence of that other appalling campus phenomenon, binge drinking. In my army years I knew the occasional man who drank straightforwardly to get drunk, usually after getting a "Dear John" letter or some other setback. But I never knew groups of men to set out collectively to drink until they dropped. Some students, I am told, get drunk on a Wednesday or a Thursday evening, depending on their course schedule the next morning, "in preparation for the weekend."

In that sad decade between 1965 and 1975 my own sights were set primarily on bringing the larger Kenyon into being, particularly on the expansion of the faculty. It was universally known that President Caples was giving me a free hand with the faculty, even though final decisions on appointment and tenure were his. The one restriction on me that I was never able to ignore was that imposed by the continuing financial crisis. That came into its fullest focus in the late 'sixties when the College was denied any further credit by local banks, a cold water shock for all of us. Fortunately for our plans, the head of a Mount Vernon bank was able to convince his board to bale us out, but the chilling effect of that near-death experience stayed with us for a very long time.

For me that meant that, as I sought to build the faculty to larger functioning size, I had to be content to appoint, in the main, low-cost brand-new Ph.D.s and some who were "all but dissertation." That would not have been the difficulty that it was, if we had not been compelled to bring on board a very large number of newcomers in such a short span of time. In a department which had three or four new members over a three-year period, doubling its size, there could not be the mentoring of the Chalmers years; the senior members were incapable of providing it to so many. I found it difficult to continue emphasizing, as Chalmers had done, the undergraduate origins of recruits to the faculty. Though we added in those years some very distinguished members, including some who had been undergraduates at strong liberal arts colleges like Amherst, Haverford, Oberlin, Lawrence, and Antioch, we brought in, too, young faculty members who were altogether products of large universities. I must hasten to say that some of those took to Kenyon like ducks to water, as I had done, but for others the adjustment was impossible.

The trustees had given me permission a year before the first female students arrived to appoint women to the faculty. I recall with great clarity interviewing our first appointee, Harlene Marley, who was also the first woman to be granted tenure. She would in time prove to be a superb department chair and a model of the professional woman. Our success rate with women who followed was about the same as that with men; for some single women as for some single men Gambier continued to be, in the words of my French colleague of yesteryear, "a difficult place to be not marry-ed." I can believe it must be still. For some other women Kenyon seemed still haunted by its "men's college" past; some of the structures of the place, including the fraternities, spoke loudly of that history. Evaluations of their work may have been colored by our expecting them to fit themselves to our idea of a college's priorities and its functioning. There is no denying the fact that, until just a short time before those women joined us, Kenyon had been a place where it was thought, in the words of the trustees, that women "would destroy the ambience of the classroom."

In my addresses to the members of the College, as in my interviewing of candidates for faculty positions, I sought to keep before the community in the years of our great expansion and thereafter, the Chalmers model of the essential college, the more as I sensed that the department was taking the place of the College in some faculty thinking and as younger faculty cleaved to the university model they had grown up with. I made a crucial mistake in those years, which promoted the centrifugal forces that were working their power on us.

Ascension Hall had soon felt the strains of our growth. We had had early to call on some faculty members to share offices and even then we could not possibly accommodate the projected growth. Hindsight argues that I should have pushed hard, even in those financially difficult years, for a new building to house faculty members, a building where the intimacies of Ascension could have been maintained. Before that I should have argued, against Caples, that the offices of the President, the Provost, and the Registrar should remain in their traditional and altogether accessible locations in Ascension. Instead I agreed that those offices should be moved into the former library building, a place that, despite its proximity to Middle Path, proved to be separate from day-by-day faculty movements. It took more effort than the casual for a faculty member to stop in to see us, though we maintained "open door" practices. The separation contributed, I am convinced, to the growing gulf between the faculty and the administration in the later Caples years.

To me alone belongs the blame for the decision to "balkanize" the faculty, as some have called it. I accepted the proposal, which began with English and Political Science, that some departments be moved into houses within the College Park, an action that meant displacing some senior faculty members and their families. Those who favored the move stressed the value to departments, in that time of rapid growth, of the socialization to the department of new, younger faculty, an argument not to be dismissed, particularly when I was anxious about those newcomers adapting to the College. I did not foresee the extent to which departments would separate themselves from the rest of the College under those conditions, though the widening gap between members of the science division and the faculty on the other side of Middle Path should have given me a clue. I continued to cling to the belief that the centripetal forces that could be exerted through the curriculum, buttressed by the example of senior faculty members, would preserve the sense of a collegiate faculty, separate as department offices might be. And that might have been the case, had not other more powerful pulls towards departmentalism come upon us. In any event, we soon had the English, History, Political Science—our three largest departments—behind white clapboard, and not long thereafter the new Department of Anthropology/Sociology occupied what had once been the chaplain's residence. The departments remaining in Ascension were quick to "balkanize" as well, with lasting and unhappy consequences for the College.

When I became Dean I resolved to remain a teaching member of the faculty. I was able to organize my time well enough that I could teach one literature course in each semester. Every other year I offered a course that had as its centerpiece Thomas Mann's *The Magic Mountain*. Some students were quick to draw parallels between the processes of Hans Castorp's education on Mann's mountain and those on Gambier's hill. In my analysis of the novel, as I did in my public statements on Kenyon and in the texts I wrote for College publications, I stressed the privilege granted one who seeks understanding: to spend time apart from the world, and thus be able to examine its processes from the distance as one cannot in the course of living in it, to be able to reflect on the purpose of life and knowledge. Philander Chase and Gordon Chalmers were right in their belief that the crucial four years of undergraduate learning should be spent in detachment from the everyday world. Several generations of Kenyon students called Gambier "the magic mountain," a name that stuck until there was conscious effort to be rid of it after I had left the College. Certainly the place worked its liberating magic with a majority of students and faculty members.

Yet, as the years moved on and the number of newcomers to the faculty swelled, I was concerned enough about the loss of collegiality that I sought a way to seek to strengthen it among the older faculty and develop it among the young. I remember being visited in my office by one of the new members, an associate professor of mathematics who had served in other institutions for a couple of decades before coming to Kenyon. He wanted to tell me, in a perfectly friendly way, that I was the first person ever to suggest to him that he had any other responsibility, as a faculty member, than to teach courses in mathematics. I had talked of the extra-departmental role, not only to him, but to all the new faculty in one way or another. How many others, I wondered, had embraced with him the larger responsibility?

Supported by a grant I obtained from the Lilly Endowment in the early 'seventies, I introduced a two-week summer program for my colleagues, which had so many successes that I have often wished the College could have maintained it as a continuing program after the Lilly money ran out. It was an idea for faculty development that ran counter to what is usually assumed under that rubric, which is in effect an extension of the individual's graduate research. Mine was to develop people as members of a collegiate faculty. For three summers, enough to have all members of the faculty participate (though none was required to do so), leaders respectively from the sciences, the social sciences, and the arts/humanities conducted discussions of the College's purposes, the salient features of the divisions' work, the role of the faculty member in the liberal arts college, the interdependence of studies, the need for synthesizing knowledge and understanding, and the like. Discussions were based on readings chosen by the leaders, though some were proposed by the participants themselves as the days moved forward. Except for a few introductory words on the first day, I kept myself out of the sessions, the more to promote the colleague-to-colleague sense I wished the sessions to have. The only requirement of participants was that they write an assessment within a month after the sessions, to be seen only by me. Those reports were most reassuring. The magic mountain was winning converts. I was encouraged by the candor and honesty with which the reports were written, many a one confessing that he or she had never recognized that some of the questions existed. I shall never forget the summing up by a young science division member: "I am no longer afraid of my colleagues."

Alas, for every advance that we seemed to make through those summer sessions, we seemed to lose ground because of the behaviors and utterances of the President. Not long after the College opened in the fall of 1971, Caples was asked to serve on President Nixon's Pay Board. Telling us of the board's approval of his accepting the invitation, he emphasized that he had served every President since Roosevelt and did not want to break his record. Sam Lord tried to argue that, with women not yet established in Gambier and with the building of new residences still under way, we could not afford the President's absence. Caples made light of those concerns, saying that the proposed schedule for the Pay Board would allow him to be in Gambier on weekends; he could take care of whatever matters needed his attention then. The trustees had already decided that I would be acting president in his absence. There was no dissuading him. Caples, I fear, had already come to think that in Gambier he was a large frog in far too small a pond. He missed rubbing shoulders with the great and powerful of the world from which he had come; the invitation promised an opportunity for him to recapture that.

Not least among our concerns, though nobody voiced it to the President or the board, was that Caples was not going to be raising the money the College continued desperately to need. From the beginning of our staff discussions in 1963 we had emphasized to one another and, eventually, to the trustees, that Kenyon needed to increase its endowment dramatically, if it were to be the institution we wanted it to be. Dear to the hearts of all of us who were teaching was the hope that a larger endowment would allow the College to restore the Chalmers scholarship programs, bringing better and more highly motivated students in larger numbers. Besides there were much needed new facilities for the arts and athletics, buildings not included in the first stages of construction. To the President belonged the task of leading fund drives, of making calls on Lilly, Ford, and other endowments, of rallying the alumni at meetings across the country. Caples's decision to go to Washington shattered our hopes. He would never become the money raiser we had imagined him to be.

The news that the President would absent himself from the College was devastating to the faculty. They were shocked at what seemed to them his cavalier attitude towards his office and his responsibilities, particularly in such a time of crucial change. A semester with an acting president, faculty members everywhere know, is a time on a campus when nothing gets accomplished. Even wholly sympathetic senior members of the faculty were at a loss to understand how Caples could bring himself to leave when the College was in such a period of transition. They knew that the administration was already stretched thin and that Kenyon's very existence was riding on the successful completion of the program of expansion we had begun. Caples seemed suddenly like Lund revisited.

He was gone throughout the first semester, not making it back to Gambier on some weekends, too distracted when he did appear to do any good. Despair grew as it became increasingly uncertain how long his tour of duty there would last; he showed no interest in cutting it short. When I was briefly in his company he would talk more of Washington than of the College. After Christmas his full-time service ended and for the next fifteen months he was gone sporadically, usually for three or four days at a time, once or twice a month. His heart, clearly, was in Washington.

Something happened that altered Caples drastically. He was a different man when he returned to his office. Some have thought that it was the slight stroke he suffered, though I have believed it was his Washington stay. I have guessed that he felt enlarged there, and reduced whenever he came back to Gambier. He seemed to resent being back with us. He had lost interest in the College's long-term plans, particularly in its need for endowment funds. Now he seemed to hover over our offices, finding fault with this, blaming us for that. Was he, I have often wondered, seeking to dispel his sense of his own failures in office by seeking to hold underlings responsible for whatever wasn't going well? Tom Edwards, Dean of Students, suffered particularly at Caples's hands, often enduring insults in staff meetings. Why Edwards became the *bête noire*, I have never understood, but it seemed clear to everybody that, when Caples decided to bring in an outsider as Vice President for Student Affairs over Edwards, his sole interest was in humbling him.

Just as he had soured on Edwards, Caples had soured on the faculty. When he was new in office he often sang the faculty's praises and sought to show his respect for them. Now, back in Gambier full time, he seemed to be trying his best to alienate them. He called them lazy and disloyal. He had become, for no really understandable reason, an enemy of the tenure system, arguing in public that granting tenure to somebody after seven years guaranteed a lack of commitment after that. He demanded that I develop for him a tenure plan that would, like Yale's, be based on a ten-year probationary period; I was able to dissuade him from advancing it to the board. Faculty friends came to me bewildered, but I was able to offer them neither comfort nor explanation for his behaviors. Tensions between him and me grew, as he imagined that I had turned the faculty against him, the more so after he suddenly declared that he would stay on as President for one year longer than the six of his first declaration. When word of this got out, there were groans all across the College.

While on other fronts things were going very well for Kenyon, with the student body rising close to our target figure and with the operating budget finally in balance, Caples had become an ogre in the institution. We were afraid of his temper; we shuddered at some of his off-the-cuff utterances; we wondered which of us might be the next Edwards, to be downgraded, to be insulted. The worst day of my month was the Monday of faculty meeting, for I never knew just what affront the faculty might suffer from Caples that day. More and more he seemed like an angry father addressing his unruly children. Sad to say, he claimed to be speaking for the trustees and all the staff when he voiced his dissatisfactions with the faculty.

Caples saved the worst for his last faculty meeting, when, in the presence of a bewildered Lord Kenyon, on a rare visit to the College that bears his family's name, he gave the faculty a farewell tongue lashing. He must surely have recognized that everybody in that room despised him in that moment. It was a terribly sad ending to a time which had opened with such promise.

Chapter VIII
Independent Contractors

When I think back on the Caples years, it is his first few years in office that I most readily recall. I am glad of that. It would be ungrateful, to say the least, to have the lasting memory of him be the bully of his later term. He deserves better. He stepped in when Kenyon desperately needed him, leaving behind a life in Chicago that had obviously been dear to his heart. He pushed through the plan for the coming of women and led us through years of national turmoil that most of us shudder to look back on. It should also be said on his behalf that he tried strenuously, using his wide contacts, to bring an African American to the faculty, but the competition for minority Ph.D.s was intense and his efforts failed. I blame myself for not having done a better job of positioning myself between him and the faculty in the last bitter years.

A minor source of friction between him and me towards the end was my having been invited to become a member of the board of consultants of the National Endowment for the Humanities. I had been careful to ask his permission to serve, even as I had asked his permission before that to serve on NEH committees that evaluated grant proposals. Though he had raised no objection on either occasion, he seemed to find a cause for a little grumble each time I informed him that I should be away on the weekend. I limited myself to two consultancies a year and visited client colleges, whenever possible, when Kenyon was not in session. Consulting gave me perspective on Kenyon, as well as providing me with a considerably broader understanding of what was going on in higher education. It was particularly rewarding to be involved in the efforts being made to restore the humanities disciplines. The Endowment had launched its consulting service when colleges began to recover from the upsets of the 'sixties and as humanities departments sought to reclaim their prominence in the undergraduate curriculum. No other set of studies had come under the sustained attack the humanities suffered. Though physics departments knew the stigma of physics allegedly having been harnessed to the production of exotic weaponry, the sciences, by and large, were not dismissed as irrelevant. The sciences, clearly, were not "over thirty," working on the cutting edge of research as they were. Some of the social sciences were decried, the traditional study of history in particular being ridiculed, but sociology, Marxist economics, and radical political science courses became the favorites of protesters, at least of those who were willing to grant that any form of organized study had value. The arts, in an age of neo-Romantic glorifying of self-expression, flourished as the media of the decade. (There was a time in the 'sixties when both the National Endowment for the Arts and NEH were granting support to guerilla theater productions.) The humanities, however, except where their professors joined the radical move to embrace only the present moment, were nearly shown the door. The number of students majoring in English and other literatures, in philosophy, religion, and Classics declined drastically across the land, while requirements in traditional humanities courses were slashed or completely abandoned.

Recovering slowly from the shock, some colleges began to consider some restoration of form in their corporate lives, and professors of the humanities were in the forefront of such efforts. (The sciences, continuingly dependent on having a "ladder" of courses, where students had to master A and B before they could tackle C and D, retained their structures through it all.) Though the journals and the *Chronicle of Higher Education* had prepared me for much that I found in other colleges and universities, I was nonetheless surprised at the extent to which the humanities had been reduced, far beyond anything we had known at Kenyon. It became clear to me that in many a college there had been simmering doubts about the worth of the humanities that were not directly related to the protests against the Vietnam War. They were seen as part of a past that might better be forgotten, their subject matters the products of "dead white males," their concerns the hobbies of an elite. They didn't suit the materialistic tone or the situational ethics that were ever more prominent in our society.

I always made a point of inquiring of professors of non-humanities disciplines, particularly members of science divisions, about their perception of the humanities in their colleges and in the education of their students. Responses were, not surprisingly, mixed. Some were not eager to see the humanities given prominence, believing they were no longer rigorous disciplines. Others acknowledged having developed some useful skills in thinking and writing in required humanities courses. Then there were the ones who gave me joy, men and women whose lives had been enriched by literature, history, and philosophy, after their eyes had been opened by skilled teachers. It always came back to their memory of teachers, as it did when I interviewed students about their perceptions. In far too many instances those who found fault with the humanities, whether faculty members or students, were those whose encounters with humanities departments had been in what were remedial courses, making up for what they should have learned in high school. They had not made discoveries, they had not found different modes of thinking nor new worlds of ideas or experience.

No consultant should carry with him a standard remedy or a "one size fits all" proposal. And, contrary to what members of faculties sometimes imagined on my arrival at their college, NEH had no agenda, no particular notion of the humanities we were to advance. I prepared myself always by reading the institution's catalogue and student handbook, seeking to know what its ambition was for its members. Needless to say, I sometimes found a large gap between the statement of purpose and the reality of the institution's life. I often found gaps, too, between what the authors of proposals to NEH were seeking and what some of their colleagues wanted. One plain effect of the 'sixties was to create a gulf between traditionalists and the new breed of faculty who had been graduate students in the revolution. Though I must hasten to say that the division was not always one of age. There were a few traditionalists among the young, particularly among the young who had graduated from liberal arts colleges, and there were nihilists among older faculty members, those who had seen their advantage in chaos. It was barely possible to bring them together for discussions of questions like "What do we think it most important for students to learn in a humanities course?" Divisions ran deep, even within departments, and beyond the humanities departments there was suspicion about what institutional resources might be diverted to revive the humanities. It was nearly always impossible to identify an institutional center, a common point of reference to which all the faculty could look, from which to take a beginning for discussion of collegiate purpose. Only rarely could I find an educational philosophy understood and embraced by a majority.

One of the rewards of the consultancy I did in the middle 'seventies, at a college with "Wesleyan" in its name, was getting to know a very successful president who was in the last of his twenty-eight years in that office. He was the head of a healthy, prospering institution that could boast many fine new buildings and a competent faculty. I got to know him well enough that I felt able to ask, at our last meeting, "What was the most important decision you ever took on behalf of your institution?" Without a second's pause he answered, "Why, taking it out of the Church, of course." He was an ordained minister, not an academic, and yet he had thought it wise, given his reading of a changing world, to put away what had first defined his college: the idea of academic work done under the authority of shared values and beliefs. The President thought it important, however, that "Wesleyan" remain in the institution's name; it had a "historical value," it still meant something to prospective students. I was unable to find what that "something" was, other than the fact that the college had a Methodist chaplain. My several visits to that college had borne out what I had thought at first acquaintance, namely that the main difference between that college and the state university in the same city was one of size.

Such was my experience in most of the colleges I served. In a Catholic college in New York State I asked faculty members and students whether there was anything except the crucifix on every classroom wall which spoke to its being Catholic. Nobody could think of an example. Other colleges that had once talked of the values they taught had stricken such references from their catalogues. "Church related" had come to mean "once church supported" and very little beyond that. Looking for an institutional center, I found departments sharing only the library and the computer network. Or, as one wit remarked, the plumbing system.

The 'sixties had, of course, brought a powerful questioning of inherited form and practice which had shaken the foundations of liberal arts colleges. But the changes discernible in the 'seventies had as much to do with the persuasions of those faculty members recently come from the graduate schools. They brought with them the conviction that not only their truth, but their future career, lay within the comfortably limited world of the department. When they spoke of the "profession," they did not mean teaching or education; they meant the body of those all across the land who were in their specialty. If they could not be quickly won to the ideals of liberal education and to their college's purposes, they would see their career interests being best served by ignoring as much as possible whatever lay beyond the department. Their ambition was to earn a national reputation as an authority, and it didn't matter where they drew their pay in the meantime.

My working class sensibilities had always been bruised by the cavalier attitudes of the British aristocracy towards their responsibilities—*noblesse oblige* seemed to have gone the way of the dodo—attitudes I found developing alarmingly among American academics. In the late 'seventies I interviewed for a position in English a young woman who wished me to know that she would be married by the time she came to Gambier. I thought I should remind her of the rule Kenyon had about faculty members living within five miles of the College, but she dismissed my concern, saying that that would be "no problem." Her husband-to-be was a professor in a large New York university, where he would arrange to do his teaching on Monday and Tuesday so that he could spend the rest of the week in Gambier with her. A little later I read of the famous professor who, it came to light, was simultaneously holding down full-time professorships in the Midwest and on the east coast. He was perplexed that people should find that unusual, while his defenders were quick to say that he was doing all that each institution really expected of him: leading a couple of graduate seminars and producing published research findings. A *member* of the faculty? I have heard of a faculty couple who walked away from their contractual responsibilities just a couple of days before classes were to begin. Amorality has become the norm. Sad to say, just before I left Kenyon I had to confront a professor of psychology whose cavalier attitudes towards his courses had brought complaining students to my office. At nearly every class meeting he was having students watch a film, sometimes one that ran for only ten or fifteen minutes, telling them to leave when it was done.

I found out eventually that he had organized his classes in the mornings, to be done before eleven, so that he could drive to Columbus in time to begin his second full-time job as a clinical counselor at Ohio State. Faced with challenge of his tenure, he resigned.

The great professors I knew at Kenyon, both in my young days and in later years, were men and women who had a sense of vocation. They saw students in the whole, not just as people passing through their classrooms. Teaching, advising, membership on committees of the College, and being interested in their colleagues were forms of service to a cause they believed in: the education of young people. In all my consultancies I found some professors who were similarly committed, but they wanted to tell me that they were in a shrinking minority. The young among those committed to education felt beleaguered, slighted by their careerist colleagues, sometimes even warned by a dean that they were too much interested in students. Some presidents and deans, thinking to gain publicity for their institutions, have contributed to the movement that has made the central commitment of the undergraduate college the interests of its faculty rather than the educational needs of students. I was to have the new breed defined by one of their number who told me, "We do not see ourselves as you wish to see us. We see ourselves as independent contractors. We are paid to perform a specific service, to teach a particular set of courses. All the rest is your business." I cannot dissociate his statement from my image of independent contractors hired to contribute their specialized labor to the building of a house, each doing his "thing" without any sense of the whole structure the architect has planned, not interested in knowing what the other contractors are doing.

Can faculty members with such a self-image make up even a functioning *department*? As the years have advanced since the 'seventies we have seen quarreling *between* departments become quarreling *within* departments, sometimes with a new department being created to house those who could not accommodate themselves to their fellows. We have moved from a college that first became a congeries of unrelated departments to departments which may be no more than a loose association of persons who earned graduate degrees in the same subject. Before the 'seventies were out I was to find Kenyon's Department of English unable to provide a definition of the major program in English. The Department split down the middle, six on each side. The traditionalists held to the view that there was a body of works in verse and prose that could and should be historically ordered into something called English literature; that body included the works of authors universally considered great, among them Chaucer, Shakespeare, Milton. Those who majored in English should have courses on those authors and on that ordered flow. The others dissented. "English literature" was a fiction created by professors and nothing was gained by studying works in a pattern. They would not accept the greater importance or worth of any author and would not even grant that there was a single work of literature that should be read by every major. Their view, to which their wearied colleagues eventually yielded, was that an English major was a student who had taken a certain number of courses taught by professors of the Department, whatever those professors might choose to teach. (Today, with a slightly tighter definition, the student majoring in English must take work in six of nine "areas," Shakespeare being one "area" to be opted for—or avoided.)

The centrifugal forces have worked their way the more with the change in the character of the department chair. Formerly thought of and often called the "head" of the department, serving at the pleasure of the president and usually for many years, the chair today is any member of the department taking a turn as the department's "facilitator," for only two or three years. An egalitarian notion has displaced a constitutional one, with the result that the department's concerns are not communicated consistently to the administration, while the administration's concerns do not get to the members of the department. More serious is the loss of leadership. I have known departments built to significant strength over the years by effective chairs, leaders who persuaded their colleagues to a shared philosophy and a style. Without such leadership a department is never more than the sum of its parts, its curriculum being only what a given set of professors in a given year is interested in teaching. To be sure, there is enough sense of responsibility in most English departments to ensure that there will be one member of the faculty who will be competent to teach Shakespeare, but what of Shakespeare will be taught and with what emphases will not be a matter of discussion in the department.

I had told the trustees well in advance of President Caples's retirement that I should not wish to succeed him. When he left in 1975 there was a sigh of relief all across the College and hopeful anticipation with the announcement of the identity of his successor. Philip Jordan was to serve Kenyon effectively for twenty years, even while he presided over the near destruction of the Kenyon of Gordon Chalmers. A highly intelligent, literate man, Jordan brought impressive credentials to the position: graduate of a distinguished prep school, B.A. *summa cum laude* Princeton, Ph.D. in history Yale, years of teaching at Connecticut College, and Dean at that same institution for a short term. He was always generous to me and it pained me to find that I could not embrace his agenda. Jordan did not share my "magic mountain" notion of a liberal arts college; he did not see the departments working together and interdependently in the educating process; he did not think of students accomplishing a synthesis of knowledge and coming to a private philosophy. He seemed to remain a university man in a college setting, more comfortable with the clash of competing ideas than with shared purpose. He preferred to see the disciplines independent, departments developing their unique strengths and competing for the attention of students, the students hearing differing voices directed at them and eventually choosing one to make their own. Sixteen years after I had left Kenyon, Jordan was to say to an interviewer who had asked about his response to my idea of the College, "Bruce had an image of the College that, when he articulated it, had great justificatory and explanatory power. The magic mountain gave you a glimpse of eternity. What troubled the faculty was, they weren't always sure that was the facility they were at. It was inspiring, but it was not the college they wanted to attend."

What was the Kenyon "they" (i.e. the faculty who achieved tenure in his time), "wanted to attend?" It was not the Chalmers Kenyon, of course, but Jordan's, a Kenyon where the department took the place of the College in faculty thinking. Jordan wished to have his idea of departmental autonomy prevail, and he wished to recruit faculty members who cherished a university identity. Decisions about appointment and retention moved out of my office into the department's; I was no longer to initiate or have veto power in appointments. Jordan saw the Provost as a facilitator for the faculty, rather than its head; I was clearly not to have the role in the Jordan Kenyon that I had had in two previous presidencies.

Jordan unleashed the centrifugal forces that soon destroyed every trace of a collegiate center, pushing departments farther and farther apart, putting self-interest above the collective, and eventually reducing the role of the faculty member in the life of the College. Years after his departure those forces have continued to work, resulting in the eventual abandonment of the storied and beloved English 1-2, so long thought of as the cornerstone of education at Kenyon.

The new President brought with him a political agenda. He wanted Kenyon to be directly engaged with the world beyond Gambier, to mold itself in response to shifting currents in that world rather than to its traditional commitments. His first appointment was a woman, wife of a faculty member, to be, in a vaguely defined position, an "ombudsperson" for women in the College. Ms. Scott seemed at first to have no more understanding of what Jordan expected from her than we had, but she gradually found her way into being a support for women faculty and staff members, as well as a checker of official documents for sexist language and the like. Henceforth Kenyon would shape itself, not in response to its inner conviction or a philosophy of liberal education, but in response to the forces that were shaping higher education in the universities, those movements which have been collectively labeled "politically correct."

Jordan's agenda was to be much more rapidly advanced in the 'eighties by my successor, who made the political consideration the prime criterion in hiring, much to the dismay of the faculty's more conservative element. Kenyon was soon a battleground between those faculty members who held to my view of the liberal arts college and the new breed who wanted Kenyon to be a university in miniature—and an academically radical one at that.

But the die was cast, partly because the traditionalists did not have the taste for combat and bloodletting that the newcomers had acquired in their college and graduate school years. When the young man who was to become my son-in-law enrolled as a freshman two years after my departure, he made passing reference, talking to his adviser, to Gambier as a magic mountain. He was quickly told not to use the term; Kenyon was no longer "that kind of place."

Indeed it was not. The new Kenyon was a more "flatland" place, a college where there would be much more direct involvement in political and social movements in the world beyond Gambier. The new Kenyon was a place where the idea of essential studies within a structured curriculum would be abandoned, where students and faculty would be encouraged to do their own thing in a college that was to be a vehicle for social change. Not, I must very quickly state, in any extreme. Jordan was himself far too conservative to let the new breed of faculty push him into that form of institutional life. His was to be a Kenyon where political and academic radicalism would be at home, but never to the degree that tuition-paying parents would be frightened off. It might be called "radical chic," as some elitist behavior was in the 'sixties.

For some faculty members this was a change eagerly wished for; no longer would they have to think of themselves as members of the College, no longer have to endure collective faculty scrutiny of their proposed new courses. Faculty members could use their classrooms to promote their personal agendas, no matter what their professional subject matter. They could refuse the tasks of advising freshmen or involvement with student organizations. And they could choose to live fifty miles away in Columbus, the five-mile rule abandoned, and be in Gambier only two or three days a week. They could become, in short, the university breed of faculty member, which was the identity they really coveted. Too many did.

In the late 'seventies I was to be told by one young assistant professor, a man who never let anybody forget that *his* father *worked* for a living, that he hated everything I stood for. He saw me as a champion of what he considered an aristocratic tradition in education. He held me responsible for all those "rich kids" cluttering up his classes, he thought me a male chauvinist and closet racist. He said it with such intensity of feeling that there could be no doubt as to the strength of his conviction.

Change must come to a college, of course. Colleges stopped believing long ago that the study of Athens and Rome alone was sufficient to educate a man for all possibilities. They have not been strange to the need to bring in new subject matters (Kenyon introduced modern foreign languages before Harvard did), they have welcomed new technologies and techniques which promised to strengthen them. But the change of a college should be like that of the amoeba, retaining its true identity while shaping itself to altered circumstance. The new breed of faculty member we were seeing in increasing numbers in the 'seventies seemed to wish that Kenyon were not a liberal arts college. A senior man in History told me that I was seen by the younger faculty "as the last link to the Chalmers Kenyon that is no longer relevant." I saw that I was out of step with the President, out of step with the faculty of the future. I was no longer happy with Kenyon and I decided to resign my position.

One trustee, learning of my decision, feared that I was, indeed, the last link with the Chalmers Kenyon, that Kenyon from which he had graduated and which he cherished as the model for the Kenyon he wished to see live on. He persuaded his colleagues to offer me an endowed professorship in the humanities, named for the College's founder. I would teach a course or two each semester and give the rest of my time to writing and speaking about liberal education, in Kenyon's name. It was sorely tempting. But that was not the answer. If I were to stay, I would become the rallying point for those who wished to resist the President and his new Provost, for those heirs of Gordon Chalmers who did not wish to see departmentalism and illiberal education triumph. I was not going to help to split asunder the Kenyon I had loved those many years. It was time for me to go. Once again I had a happy career opportunity before me. I was contacted by a trustee chairman whose college wanted a president who would provide it with academic leadership. Once again I responded to being told that a college needed me. This time it was Monmouth College of Illinois, a Presbyterian foundation with a governing board that wanted to see liberal education resurrected in the institution. In the summer of 1980 I said my farewell to Kenyon. It was like leaving England all over again, alienated from the place that had shaped me, eager to embrace a new citizenship.

In the two decades since I left Gambier, higher education has advanced the more rapidly along the path charted in the nineteen-seventies, as the student rebels of yesteryear became tenured faculty members, seeking to make the campuses the instruments for the political and social changes they wished to see in the larger society. For them higher education was a propaganda agency for their beliefs. Whereas some faculty members of an earlier time had feared that their college might rank church membership or piety above scholarship, the new generation was eager to see ideology made a prime factor in hiring and retention. Instead of collegiality, compatibility was prized. While institutions, public and private alike, preached diversity, they practiced an increasing narrowness in their appointment of faculty members. Karl Marx replaced Plato as the thinker whose ideas were most often cited in college classrooms. Academic rigor was sacrificed to emotional response to questions. It seemed as though all that had once been central in liberal education had come under siege.

Now the liberal arts college, if it is to survive, must have a restatement of its purpose, a new commitment that goes beyond the small-scale adjustments to degree requirements which some institutions have undertaken in recent years. It needs a powerful metaphor that will reorient it to Jefferson's expectation of it. It needs to show that there is a great and compelling purpose to the pursuit of knowledge.

Chapter IX
The Purpose of Knowing

Though *The Magic Mountain* provided several generations of Kenyon undergraduates with a metaphor for their college years, it was not in that novel that I found the metaphor which has undergirded all my thinking about liberal education. Rather it was in the greatest work of German literature, Goethe's *Faust*, the dramatic poem from which Thomas Mann drew the title of his novel and much else that went into the work.

Before Goethe, the Faust portrayed in both serious and popular fiction had been damned for bartering his immortal soul. Goethe made of him a sinner redeemed. To Goethe, Faust seemed to embody the tragic ambiguity that comes with occupying a place halfway between angel and animal. His Faust speaks painfully of the "two souls" that dwell within his breast, each seeking always to be separated from the other. The one tells him of the joys to be found within our earthly situation, the daily round and common task that the hymn tells us will furnish all we ought to ask. It urges him to accept his physical limitations, to seek the pleasures of home and hearth, to find happiness within a rationally ordered scheme of things where individuality must always make concessions to the demands of the group. The other soul, just as insistent, speaks of bursting the bonds of physical circumstances. It calls him to scale mountain peaks and fly over oceans. It accepts no limits to its striving and sets its selfish ambition above all the claims of reasonableness, denying any responsibility other than to itself.

Goethe, a man with a revolutionary view of the human condition, seems to have seen in Faust the spirit that might inspire a new world, the energy that might create a free society, even seeing Faust as the first representative of a new liberated humanity. While Goethe worked on his Faust drama at intervals over a long life, completing it just a few months before his death in 1832, he had written its earliest scenes several years before the American Revolution and those pages throb with the same rebellious energy and love of freedom that we know in our Declaration of Independence.

While Goethe transformed a familiar legend, he preserved many of its elements. His play begins where all before him had begun, with a medieval professor who has exhausted all the traditional paths to knowledge and who rebels against the limits that convention sets about him. The opening monologue is built upon a sustaining irony: Faust is the greatest scholar of his time, and yet, he cries out in despair, there is nothing that he could tell his students that would be of the slightest use to them! All his efforts to become expert in the university's ways have the more surely carried him away from his original goal: to understand life in its innermost working. The university is not only an ivory tower; it is a prison, a place where all experience and understanding is ordered into a deathly system. Looking about his study Faust sees the skeleton that is supposed to tell him what is man; the shelves hold bottles and vials into which nature has been distilled; his dusty books claim to contain two thousand years of human history—all of this the cruel evidence of mankind's continuing effort to know what life is by reducing it to its smallest identifiable elements. "And this," Faust moans, "this is my world!" It is not life that surrounds him, but death. Reason has made its own constructs, hoping to find in them an analogue and key to life; but these have become instead a wall that separates Faust altogether from the humanity he has wished to know in its full dimension.

Brought close to suicide by his despairing recognition that he has wasted decades of his life in futile activity, Faust concludes that he will know life only if he lives it. He must break out of his prison cell, abandon the path of reasoned inquiry, and seek knowledge in experience. He will "plunge into the rush of time, the race of events, hit or miss, pain or pleasure; just as it comes, always on the move, always doing something. It's the only way … I mean to expose myself to all the pain and suffering in the world. Nay more, I mean to experience in my own person all that is given to humanity to experience … to enlarge myself in this way to humanity's size and to smash up with the rest of humanity in the end."

Plainly there is no change of ambition here. Faust is still thinking in absolute terms of knowing all that can be known. Only now he chooses a different path to knowledge, giving preference to feeling over rationality. But such a road cannot be followed by a graybeard professor who has, as he ruefully acknowledges, "never felt at home in the world." This demands rejuvenation so that he may live and experience in his own flesh what is known to those who do not follow the university's way. This calls for magic, for Mephistopheles, and Faust does not shrink from this devil, even when Mephisto identifies himself as "the spirit which eternally negates" and as part of the chaos that everywhere prevailed before there was form in the universe.

The play moves into a second phase of irony, for Faust, delivered from one form of bondage, is as quickly delivered into another. He comes eventually to understand that, whatever the value of individual experience, it is ultimately more confining than his office.

A young man again, thanks to magic, Faust falls in love and lives through a series of tragic circumstances. Love, as his beloved Gretchen understands it, can be wholly realized only within a set of societal and religious forms which Faust finds as deadly and threatening to his ego as those of the university. His passion drives him to do violence to Gretchen's world, even while he recognizes that what he cherishes in her—her beauty of soul, her serenity, her chastity, her simple honesty—comes from her being so completely at home in that world. Faust's two souls are no more reconciled out in the little world of ordinary humanity than they were in the university.

The first part of the play ends with a series of violent deaths, as others pay the price for Faust's getting to know himself through experience. Dreadfully, Gretchen is executed for having crazily murdered their bastard child after Faust has abandoned her. Faust at this stage is well characterized when he describes himself as a torrent plunging down the mountain side, undermining the hut that stands on its bank and carrying it down into the abyss below. Driven by his absolute will to know, he has no sense of knowledge having a meaning beyond the gratification of his ego. Neither in the knowing that is the arid systematizing of the university nor in the naive routine of living that is the way of the unsophisticated does Faust find *purpose*. Yet he has learned an important lesson. He has understood that he must know life both "in the rush of time … just as it comes, always on the move," and at the same time life observed dispassionately in the larger pattern—known beyond the limits of his own, private experience. And he has come to understand that he cannot know himself except by knowing others and by coming to understand the humanity that he shares with all the others who are the children of life.

As the second part of the play begins, Faust abandons the pursuit of absolute knowledge, recognizing that that is reserved for God alone. The worth of a free life must be known within the limited context of human experience. He is reassured by his sense that the purpose of knowing can be understood within the sphere of earthly existence; there is no reason to look beyond it. He does not expect to find answer, however, in Gretchen's world, within the all too limited world of the bourgeoisie. That is the world of those who are governed by others' wills and visions. They call knowledge what others impose on them as rule. They are so caught up in the routine of living that they have neither time nor desire to seek a purpose to their living.

Instead, Faust moves to the center of his society and the seat of its authority, the court of the Emperor. In that arena he looks to find the knowledge that gives direction and purpose to the larger world. But he finds only another disappointment. The court is simply Gretchen's world on a larger scale. The rulers know no more than the ruled, and their lives, no less than those of their subjects, are ordered by habit, self-interest, and blind custom. The aristocracy uses its elevated state only for greater self-indulgence and the playing of elaborate games. Without any sense of responsibility to the past or the future, the court seeks only escape from boredom. The greatest favor the newcomer can provide is a new way of killing time.

Finding nothing in the world of his own time, at either end of the social and political order, to give him any sense of knowledge's being purposefully used, Faust is drawn to ancient Greece, moving with Mephisto's powers back through the centuries to the origins of Western culture: the world of Greek mythology. This is the world that Faust has been taught to revere as the cradle of our civilization, the source of the forms that have defined Western humanity. And here he finally finds answers, something worth knowing.

First, he sees that, although the external circumstances of life change in the rush of time, there are abiding elements. People live out their lives in the presence of an eternal struggle between a will to give form, meaning, and permanence to existence and a negating, disruptive spirit that wishes always to fragment, to tear down, to destroy. At times the latter claims men's allegiance or their passions make them its slaves. Cultures rise and fall; civilizations come and go. But life in its defining features goes on.

The second truth the Greek world shows Faust is that life cannot be sustained without the forms that set limit to it and thus give it definition. Yet, if the form becomes rigid, life is immediately threatened in its ability to adapt itself to a changing environment. The forms of a society, whether the forms of its political life, its economy, its art, or social organization, are successful and life-enhancing only so long as people know their meaning and their function. Knowledge important to the welfare of the society is kept alive and transmitted by vital forms. But the knowledge is lost or rendered useless when the form loses its vitality and becomes only convention or habit.

Only now does Faust understand the lethargy and purposelessness of his own age. His society has inherited the forms the Greeks created, forms which were originally animated by Greek belief. But without the belief, the forms have become sterile. Life has become a tedious reenactment of hackneyed routines, carried on within familiar but uncomprehended patterns. Consequently people seek escape, but only in the gratification of their immediate desire. Their mode of existence has become a denial of their freedom of will.

Returning to his own time and his German homeland, Faust finds his attention arrested by the sea breaking upon the shore, for him at once a dramatic representation of that eternal struggle he has observed in the world of antiquity. "The water comes creeping up, barren in itself, to spread its barrenness wherever it goes, in every hole and corner. Now it has flooded that desolate stretch of land and there the waves run riot. Then they recede and nothing has been gained. It nearly drives me mad to see the elements so uncontrolled, wasting their energy so blindly." And with this Faust announces to Mephistopheles what he is resolved now to make his life's work: to build dikes and claim new land from the ocean, setting his own energies against the elements. And he knows that he can succeed, for he can use his knowledge of the ocean to tame it: "However much it rages, a slight rise can divert it, a slight drop can pull it down."

There is one obstacle to Faust's plan: the Emperor owns all the land along the shore. Faust will have to gain a grant of land from him, for services rendered, and at just the right time Faust has an opportunity to serve the ruler. For there is civil war in the realm. A counter-emperor, a pretender to the throne, has raised his banner and the Emperor is in desperate need of allies. That Goethe placed the rebellion in the same dramatic context as Faust's encounter with the ocean tells us that he intended a parallel: the uprising is no less an expression of elemental power, no less destructive, no less in need of containment by appropriate forms than the ocean is. And to understand Goethe's intention altogether, we must look at the way in which the war transforms the emperor. Challenged by a would-be destroyer, the moribund institutions of the Empire—court, army, government—are revitalized, as is the Emperor himself. "A counter-emperor has a very real value," the monarch says cheerfully. "It makes me feel at last that I am the true one. I only dressed in armor before as a uniform, but now it is converted to a higher purpose."

Faust uses Mephisto's minions to build his dikes, forcing back the sea and creating a new land. Yet, at a great age and the monarch of all he surveys, he finds himself still unfulfilled. For once again he has served only his own ego in testing his knowledge against the elemental energies of nature.

The Purpose of Knowing

There remain two final steps to his fulfillment—and, we may insert, to his satisfying Goethe's conditions for his redemption. First, he renounces all magic and makes himself at last independent of Mephistopheles. Then, as he enjoys the last few moments of his existence in complete freedom, he recognizes that his new land must be an America, the home of a free people, a population not of his servants, but his equals in understanding and energy. If it is not that, it will be quickly reclaimed by the ocean after his death. His vision will be lost, the evidence of his life will be washed away. With his physical vision gone, the light of his spirit burns brighter than ever, as he gives definition to the great truth his mind now grasps. He utters these last words, his magnificent final vision before death claims him:

> I will open up space for many millions to live—
> to live not safe from all danger, but safe enough.
> The fields will be green and fruitful,
> for humans and for animals,
> both of them quickly at home on this new land,
> all settled in close up against the dike that
> many hands have built with fearless toil.
> Within the dike life will be a paradise.
> No matter how much the floods rage and mount
>   to the dike's very brink;

no sooner will they nibble at it, threaten it,
than all the people will as one run to plug the breach.
Now I find this altogether enthralling.
This is the final conclusion that wisdom affords us:
the only person who deserves freedom
is the one who has to fight for it every day.
And it is knowing this that we shall all live our lives, young and old,
with danger at our door.

In this work of many powerful and complex symbols, none is more important to Goethe's intention than the dike, his metaphor for the purpose of knowing. It is first of all the emblem of Faust's completed life, the evidence of his having successfully set his creative energy and will to give form against the devilish forces in nature. The dike and the land within it are what of his ego will survive his physical existence. In creating the dike Faust has asserted that to be human, not merely animal, is to wish self-consciously to be more than the captive of time's onward rush and the relentless forces of change. The dike proclaims that the human will, guided by knowledge, can confidently set its energies and vision against seemingly overwhelming forces.

A second, and for Goethe no less important, value of the dike is that it is the form through which Faust's knowledge can be translated into knowledge for all who come after him. Goethe measures the worth of Faust's free life, in the end, by the value to the human race of his vision. In the lines I have just quoted, Faust's utopian land, within the dike's perimeter, is not proposed as a place where men and women will live like so many contented cows cropping luxuriant grass. The free soil will be a paradise, a new Garden of Eden, yes. From the chaotic ocean will come the breeze which keeps fresh the air that would otherwise stagnate, the rain that feeds the soil. But the Eden will be that only so long as people live "close up against the dike," living with one eye, so to speak, always upon the precarious barrier between themselves and destruction. For the dike is not merely a monument to the grandeur of the human spirit, the declaration that this land has been won for habitation. It is a reminder of the dangerous chaos that is always there beyond the dike and just as much a warning of the threat to civilization as it is civilization's proud boundary marker. Paradise and chaos live in tension with each other; the dike transmits the energies of human will and elemental forces pitted against each other. What makes a free life within the dike precious, what gives it worth, is the knowledge of the threat to it from without. To forget that freedom has its source in the struggle against nihilism is to lose it.

But more. On what else, besides that knowledge, does Faust say freedom depends? It is purchased by the willingness of every person to give up present interest and rush to plug any breach. The inexhaustible ocean, Faust knows, will hurl its waves ever higher, always threatening the dike. Only by every generation's knowing the truth of the dike and rebuilding it to cope with the elements' greater pressures will the sustaining form be kept vital and the society survive. We may confidently believe that Goethe intended the dike, in *this* metaphorical function, to represent all the forms of a free society—political, social, artistic, religious.

There is much in Goethe's play which argues that every vital society needs Faust's two souls, brought together in creative tension. The society of the dike proposes the harmony realized. The containing, stabilizing, form-giving "soul" is prevented from sinking into torpor by the striving ambition of the "soul" that is ever ready to look upon the challenge of the elemental. The energies and passion of that second "soul" are in turn restrained and turned to the good by the altruistic impulse of the first. There is challenge enough in this world, Faust has learned, and there will be new dikes for every generation of Fausts to build. For the dike is not the rigid structure of the crustacean's shell; it is the "perimeter" of the amoeba—flexible, adapting, life-sustaining in its ability to change with changing circumstance. Within such a perimeter a free nation's soil may be enlarged again and again as a place "for many millions to live" and a place where a Faust in any age might know the supreme joy of standing as a free man "on a free soil with a free people." To live within such a world is to recognize limitation, to know the finite as the essential condition of human existence, and yet never to feel imprisoned by that knowledge.

For what Goethe insists is that there is but one fundamental choice given to all those who claim the name human. It is to choose between living in a prison or living free. The purpose of our knowing is to see the many shapes that the prison cell may take, to understand the price of freedom, and to know how to choose between imprisonment and freedom.

Goethe's powerful metaphor should be embraced by the American college that seeks to work within a tradition of educating men and women to freedom, the tradition of liberal education. Such a college will not wish to proclaim that "knowledge will set you free" and then offer its students what the university afforded Faust: the imprisoning forms of fragmented information; the simple coexisting of separate compartments of factual knowledge; the subordinating of an interest in humanity to the university's own self-contained little world. Neither will such a college wish to suggest that knowing something worth knowing means understanding only how to satisfy the appetites and ambitions of the individual ego.

The essential college will have all the qualities of Goethe's dike, being society's visible bulwark against barbarism and its best response to the negative forces within humankind. Proposing permanence of a kind that civilized men and women may cherish, it will at the same time see itself needing to be shaped by every generation. With its own integrity, it will nevertheless willingly adapt itself to the changing wind and waves. It will offer, indeed, the example of what all society's forms must be capable of, as it mediates between the security of the familiar and established and the challenge of the unknown. Tautly drawn like the dike, it will transmit the tensions between what society needs to know for its future and what it must do to preserve the best of its past. The college's vitality will depend on its being always in touch with what is on both sides of the dike. It will never shut itself off from society's hearth and home in order to occupy itself solely with the waves breaking on the shore. Neither will it turn its back on the dangerously unfamiliar in order only to restate the virtues of traditional knowledge.

Because it believes that freedom requires making thoughtful choices, the essential college will wish its students to know that freedom is not license, even as it will wish them to know that slavery may take many forms. Men and women may be imprisoned by a political or economic system, but they may also be shut within a profession or a life that has become only routine. Indeed, the college will wish to demonstrate that even the liberal arts can become a prison cell, if they come to be ends in themselves, instead of being used to illuminate the lives of those who are drawn to them. Students need to be reminded every day that the prison cell that is the most confining and which is, at the same time, the one we are most likely to be held within, is an all too limited sense of ourselves. The only way to be released from the captivity is to be constantly in touch with the dynamic range of human potential. We need Thoreau to remind us that to remain at Walden Pond is to deny ourselves involvement in a thousand other lives. The liberal arts can be our mode of access to those many other lives and our way throughout our lives of keeping ourselves always close up against the dike. For only there, in close touch with those activities that proclaim the worth of a free life, will a college's students and its graduates be reminded that what is worth knowing is that which will secure and enhance the lives of others as well as one's own. The college will proclaim that the greatest reward men and women can find in their earthly existence is in joining others to build and rebuild the forms and institutions through which freedom-loving people have sought to propose the values they most cherish and wish their children to inherit.

Chapter X
The Liberal Arts Beleaguered

In appealing for a return to an education for the understanding and use of freedom, I do not underestimate the challenges to the liberal arts college. Most liberal arts colleges have known existences that, if not always hand to mouth, have been anything but carefree. Most of them have known financial crises; nearly all of them have had a period of frozen salaries and budget slashing. For some there have been times when it seemed as though the college might soon breathe its last. There have, in fact, been moments in our national history when observers thought confidently to forecast that liberal arts colleges would soon be a thing of the past. Though those prognosticators were of course wrong in the main, they were sadly right in many a particular instance.

Once again liberal arts colleges are sorely beleaguered, as students and their parents seem ever less likely to find the cost differential between the state university and the private college understandable and acceptable. The colleges are having to try very hard to make a case for their place in higher education, forced more and more, ironically enough, to imitate the practices of the very universities that threaten their existence.

The first fact of life for a college is that it must attract students if it is to live. For the vast majority of colleges, the time is long past when income from student tuition could be regarded as a minor item in the budget, with the major sources of income being a founding church, an endowment, or trustees passing the hat. One sure way of measuring a college's economic health is to see what percentage of its income has to come from student tuition; in the poorest colleges that percentage may be as high as eighty or ninety. Even reasonably well endowed institutions will likely have to bring in a freshman class with half of them full-tuition payers. Only the super rich, places like Amherst or Grinnell, can admit students without reference to their ability to pay, assuring them that, if they are admitted, their financial need will be met. For most other colleges a juggling act goes on, as financial aid directors seek to produce a "package" that will include state and federal grant monies, college grants, loans, campus jobs, and the amount the student should be expected to contribute. Most admissions officers today will admit that the shape of that package is likely to determine what the student's choice of college will be. Not surprisingly, parents have been known to approach a session with the financial aid officer as they would approach the car dealer, haggling to get a greater discount, even of fifty dollars. Some presidents joyfully greet a larger freshman class than the previous year had brought, even while they have to think painfully of the endowment income that had to be spent to recruit its members.

Such competition for students has drastically altered the ways in which colleges present themselves to the world. Admissions officers, with the exception of those at the highly prestigious colleges and universities, are no longer gatekeepers, letting in only a chosen few. Instead they are sales and recruiting officers, armed with expensively produced materials that promise more than any college could possibly deliver. Their representatives tour territories like so many old-time sales reps, promoting their college with high school guidance counselors, seeking to hold interviewing sessions with the college bound. Every college has its website on the internet, most of them looking as though they had been created by the same public relations office in Chicago or Los Angeles. There is a great emphasis on what admissions directors refer to as "curb appeal," the manicured look that a campus must have if it is to draw in the parents who are taking the senior-year campus tour with their children. I have heard a surprisingly large number of parents say that they "didn't bother to get out of the car," after taking a sweeping look at a campus.

Competition is so intense that it has produced ugly instances of a college's recruiters denigrating another college: "Oh, you wouldn't want to go there, they have …." A few years ago high schoolers who had applied to one Illinois college were phoned by recruiters from a half dozen other colleges, who urged those students to withdraw their applications, saying that it wasn't a safe place to be. A student had been murdered on the campus and its rivals were hastening to find advantage. Two of them were in the same academic consortium as that college.

The worst consequence of the competition among colleges is the coddling of students. That coddling takes a variety of forms, but it is present in greater or lesser degree everywhere. I quote again the remarkably prescient statement made by President Truman's commission on higher education, which said in 1947, "The student and his rounded development will be at the center of institutional activities and subject matter at their periphery." Even the members of that commission could not have foreseen just how "rounded" the contemporary student would expect his development to be, but they came very close to the truth in their prediction that academic work would be subordinated to what is commonly called "student life." In an October 5, 2003, column *The New York Times* asserted that "the competition for students is yielding amenities once unimaginable on college campuses, spurring a national debate over the difference between educational necessity and excess." The state universities have set the pace, spending vast amounts of tax money—$120 million at Ohio State, for example—to create recreational centers that are health club/country club/beach resort/nightclub rolled into one. Given the expectations of students who have been pampered at home and in high school, a university cannot consider such facilities frills, says the President of the University of Vermont. Every campus has to have them. And so the little private colleges are desperately following suit, sometimes taking on staggering mortgages in the process, for it is impossible to compete if one has a facility that costs less than, say, twenty million. Perhaps the next step was inevitable: massages, pedicures, and manicures for students at the University of Wisconsin/Oshkosh and elsewhere, jacuzzis, water slides, a theme park, a snack bar in the library, free doughnuts in the hall where final exams are being written. Asked by a *Times* reporter to say what would be the "outer limit" in amenities a university would provide, a representative of the University of Houston said that she couldn't think there was one, so intense is the competition among institutions, private and public. The rich—particularly the tax-supported rich—get richer, while the poor try desperately to keep up with the Joneses.

The perceived need to provide every service to students that can be dreamed up has led to a remarkable expansion of student affairs staffs, the private colleges again following the lead of the public universities. That has come about in part, it must be acknowledged, because faculty members have so often wished to withdraw from activities that once were theirs: academic advising, serving as advisers to student publications and clubs, helping with minor sports like golf and tennis. Deans of students have been quick to take up the slack, greatly expanding their staffs. Today there are associate and assistant deans for housing, for minority affairs, for international students, career development, academic support, community service, student activities, academic advising. Their number keeps growing as new student needs are discovered or invented. One alumnus, observing developments at his alma mater in the past decade, suspected there must be an "associate dean for excuses," so much did the tone of the place suggest the possibility.

Nobody is quite willing to use the word "customer" out loud, but in their eagerness to satisfy student expectations colleges seem to have adopted a "customer is always right" approach to both prospective and enrolled students.

That all of this translates into ever higher bills for parents is obvious. In my first year at Kenyon my salary, without fringe benefits, was roughly equal to the sum of comprehensive tuition and fees paid by four students. If a beginner at Kenyon today were paid by that same formula, his salary would be around $150,000. That his salary is instead around $38,000 means that a lot of student money is going to things other than faculty salaries. It will likely be going to pay for a resident physician or at least a clinic with a full-time nurse, resident psychological counselors, a relentlessly expanding computer center, more extensive academic services like a larger library, to say nothing of those associate and assistant deans. A college today is a far more complex enterprise, and far more expensive to run, than was the college of fifty years ago. It is that in part because students and parents expect it to be, want it to be. And, yes, there's a lot of money going into coddling.

But the worst kind of student coddling today is not detectable as a line item in the budget. It is coddling in the form of lower demands on students, lower expectations. By now everybody must have heard of grade inflation, a phenomenon all through our system, from first grade to graduate school. A Princeton University survey in 2003 of Ivy League Universities, M.I.T., Duke, and Stanford found that forty-four to fifty-five percent of all grades awarded were A. Similar figures, I can confidently say, would be found elsewhere. The once "satisfactory" C is now viewed by students as the equivalent of failure; it isn't the honor grade their high school experience has taught them to expect for little effort. Woe to the faculty member who gives less than a B, for it will lead at least to a demand from the student that there be reconsideration and negotiation for a higher grade. It may lead to an abusive phone call from an angry parent, who will claim that the grade is going to ruin his kid's chance at med school or Phi Beta Kappa. It may lead to a call from the Provost, who fears that the family will hire a lawyer to charge the college with false advertising, the college having said that professors would be "accessible." Doesn't that mean accommodating, forgiving, open to suasion?

Partly because so many students are entering colleges these days unused to serious study and often not ready for college-level work, faculty members have been pressured to lower their expectations. I know of faculty members who are assigning only about half the reading they assigned when they began their careers thirty years ago and even then, they tell me, many students fail to do all the reading. It is all part of what has been called the "dumbing down of America," the widespread acceptance of the notion that students at every level should get by with a lot less effort, a lot less seriousness. The saddest result is that many students actually believe that they are very good students (even when they know that they haven't been working), because the As and Bs on their record tell them that they are. What their B+ average says, in truth, is that they are merely mediocre.

While everybody talks about grade inflation, nobody seems to know what to do about this unhappy legacy of the egalitarian 'seventies. Harvard has justified the A average of its senior class by the explanation that, after all, Harvard admits only A students to start with. At lesser institutions excuse is found in the unwillingness of the faculty to jeopardize their students' chances of getting into the graduate school of their choice; it is a well known fact that a candidate doesn't get to the admissions committee unless his grade average is good enough to get him past the secretary who does the first sorting.

Has this inflation of grade expectations led inevitably to the worst form of coddling I have witnessed? In some colleges now students are given the opportunity to keep their permanent record cards free of evidence of their failure or near failure. The college may simply not show on the record that a student was enrolled in a course that he failed. It may grant the student the right to withdraw from a course *on the day before the final examination*, without the record card showing that the student was ever enrolled. College Woebegone, where all the grades are high and all the students are above average!

There will be no end to this until the Ivy League lends its prestige to a sustained effort to return higher education to the recommended curves and distributions of grades that were common when I entered the profession. The little colleges would not dare be in the van of such a movement. But there can be no talk of a return to academic rigor and serious work until the problem of grade inflation is addressed.

Sad to say, the college's small classes have not protected it from the cheating that is such a feature of higher education now. National polls show that a very high percentage of students have cheated in at least one course; some of them admit to cheating habitually. The internet, with its readily available essays and term papers for purchase, has made the detection of academic dishonesty more difficult, for those who provide these "services" have become increasingly skilled in making their products look like the work of freshmen or what have you. But, again, the evidence suggests that the colleges are not doing all that they might to attack this assault on their integrity. I know of instances where repeat offenders have been allowed to graduate with their class, in at least one case because a dean feared a lawyer-father. Elsewhere I have been met with a shoulder-shrugging "What are we to do?" response from faculty members who have wearied of following internet trails. Dishonesty is so much the norm in our society, some say, that it is fruitless for the college to preach against plagiarism and other forms of cheating. Yet dishonesty undermines everything the liberal arts college has stood for.

Once again competition with the universities for the "customer" whose every shopping wish must be met accounts, at least in part, for the enormous increase in the kind and number of courses offered in colleges today. Overseas programs have grown geometrically, the Kenyon Catalogue advertising "dozens of programs in Africa, Asia, Australia, and New Zealand, Europe, Latin America and the Caribbean, and the Middle East." Most colleges will offer a similar menu, all of them granting that the "meaningful experience" the student will have overseas will be the equivalent of work done on campus. I will grant that virtually every student who has talked to me about an overseas semester has wished to assure me that he or she had a "wonderful time," but the account of the semester seems indistinguishable from what I used to hear from students who spent a summer backpacking around Europe. The difference is credit towards the degree and reinforcement of the student's notion that a brief encounter is the equal of an extended engagement.

Meanwhile, back on campus the offerings of departments have exploded, as the colleges seek to offer "something for everybody" and as departments compete with one another for majors. At three small liberal arts colleges I visited this past year I found these courses being offered:

> The Anthropology of Alcohol Use
> Poverty and Social Welfare Policy
> Museum Anthropology
> Black British Cultural Studies
> Modern Poverty
> Ethnobotany
> Introduction to Children's Literature
> Trials in Early America
> Technology in American History
> The American Farm
> Women and War
> Topics in Jewish History
> Comparative Revolutions
> Psychology of Gender

Fifty years ago, I am confident, those topics would have been thought too specialized even for graduate students. I could easily have added many more to the list.

But the colleges' need to advertise curricular and experiential variety has coincided in the past twenty years with the desire of faculty members, in the university manner, to offer courses on their very special interests or, indeed, their political or social agenda. From those same colleges I culled these examples:

> Biology in Science Fiction
> Japan: Art and Idea
> Caribbean Literature and Culture
> Francophone African Literature
> Global Antifeminism
> Social Life of Food
> The Search for the Female Voice in
>   Contemporary Theater
> Contemporary Australian Fiction
> Socialism at the Movies
> The Algerian Novel
> The History of Clothing and Fashion
> Philosophy of/and/in Film
> History and Practice of the Book
> The Reception of Shakespeare in Germany
> Sensuality and Sagacity
> Queer Shakespeare

In some courses of this genre a student can expect to hear the professor reveal more of himself than the student can possibly have expected—or wished—to know. The professor may talk of his sexual awakening, his first experience with intercourse, his rejection of his parents, his turn to atheism, his divorce, his embrace of Marxism. I have invented none of this. Remarkably, faculty members who expect a college to be rigorous in following the guidelines on appointment and tenure of the American Association of University Professors (in faculty circles the equivalent of the Supreme Court), are able to ignore that same organization's strict warnings to faculty members that they not speak in their classrooms on matters on which they have no professional authority, particularly not on political questions. Yet countless class hours go into confessional unveilings and propagandizing.

The college's competition with the university for students is paralleled by its competing for faculty members and, again, with some parallels in coddling. Faculty members, too, have fewer demands placed upon them these days. They teach fewer courses than before—a prime reason for higher tuition—and they see fewer students. They get much more time off, on salary, for research and recuperation. But the most obvious example of the way in which a college bows to the demands of its faculty members is the authority it has granted them in institutional matters, particularly in letting them determine the shape of the college's working week. Students are heard to complain more and more that they have not been able to take courses they need to graduate, because so many classes are crowded into the days and hours favored by the faculty. The schedule of class meetings, like so much else these days, will have been designed to fit the faculty's wishes rather than the students' needs, with some faculty members appearing on campus only two days a week and keeping next to no office hours.

A faculty today is more likely to see itself as a political body than as a community of scholars. In most state universities the faculty is organized into a union, which usually has its own lawyers to meet with the institution's lawyers to discuss salaries and conditions of employment. Some private colleges have followed that example, the more so as the notion of the faculty member as "independent contractor" has taken hold. But even where there is no union, the faculty body is likely to see itself organized about its parochial interests rather than the college's. One of the more remarkable propositions ever put to me was, "The faculty's interests and the college's interests always coincide," an assertion that cannot stand a moment of scrutiny. But aggressive faculties have succeeded in moving the recruitment and socialization of faculty away from the president and provost into faculty committees, which routinely place faculty interests (voiced through department representatives) before collegiate interest. They have often been granted the right to debate (*sic*) the proposed operating budget for the college before it is advanced to the trustees; they have been allowed to determine the shape of the calendar, and to deny some speakers the college's platforms.

All of this can readily be traced back to the uproars of the 'sixties and 'seventies and that period's challenging of institutional forms. Trustees, eager to avoid ongoing campus upset, have yielded their authority, without demanding that the faculty accept responsibility along with their new power. The tenure system guards faculty members from any accountability for their committees' actions, even though these may seriously affect the college's life for the worse. In much faculty discourse one detects the belief that the college is organized like the federal government, with the faculty as the Congress that can hold the executive branch (the administration), and the judicial (the trustees), to its wishes by the power of its numbers and its having been elected (granted tenure). It is astonishing to find such a false analogy so widely embraced. It is just as astonishing to find college officers bowing to faculty tyranny; I was told recently by a student that her academic dean's explanation for his inability to deal with her very legitimate complaint was, "The first thing you have to understand is that the faculty runs this college."

There is an ironic twist to all this: faculties have forgotten that, back in some distant century, faculties invented deans so that they would not quarrel among themselves over administrative matters and not have to yield precious time to the mundane. Now, with deans denied the role they ought to be playing, one hears of internecine warfare as different groups of faculty members struggle for power. At the several colleges I have visited in the past few years, nearly the first thing I have heard is that faculty members are unhappy, and this at colleges where salaries are high, fringe benefits generous, and opportunities for research abundant. The evidence argues to me that the prime source of their unhappiness is their having no sense of membership, no notion of fellowship. Faculty unhappiness, it need hardly be said, does not help the college in its efforts to recruit students or win alumni support.

I have introduced this matter of faculty authority because the power that faculties have gained in the life of the college is a prime problem for trustees who would wish to see their beleaguered institution return to the modes of education and the values it once took pride in. Believing, as trustees must, that the future health of their college depends on its being a significant alternative to the university, they may find themselves confronting a faculty that is determined to have the college imitate the university as much as it is able to do so.

Then there is a relatively new problem that attaches to the recruitment and retention of faculty members: the Ph.D. spouse. In my early days in the profession there was a general nepotism rule; a college did not hire a spouse, a fact of usually little concern when academics were not so likely to be married to academics. Today 40% of married faculty members are married to academics, and one of the first questions a candidate for a faculty position is likely to ask is whether there will be an opening for his or her spouse. Large universities are often able to accommodate husband and wife teams, even in the same department, remarkably enough; they may even hold out the promise of a second position in order to recruit a prime candidate for the first. But for the small college the Ph.D. spouse poses a very real problem, particularly if the college is at some distance from a city where there are other academic institutions. I know of some happy successes with couples sharing a position, even as I have known cases where the failure of one spouse to get tenure resulted in the departure of both. It is yet another problem on top of all the others the college has to face.

There is an awful irony to the colleges' efforts to make themselves attractive to prospective students: the very things they have done or are failing to do are the source of the widespread lack of confidence in them. One hears it voiced on all sides: politicians, civic leaders, members of the professions, and above all the parents of those already in college or about to enter.

A characteristic piece of bad news for the beleaguered college comes from the business community, the world of work to which the large majority of its graduates expects to be headed and from which the college expects to derive, directly or indirectly, a large measure of financial support. On April 25, 2004, the *Chicago Tribune* ran a column headed, "Education failing to serve economy, business leaders say." The piece cites the opinions of Alan Greenspan and others, one of whom asserts, "The language skills of people from elite institutions frequently are not what they should be …. The old emphasis on the basics has gotten lost in the shuffle." The column goes on to claim that "some in the academic and business worlds are calling for a system that delivers knowledge and not just grades." A second spokesman finds "the English language skills, reading ability and mathematics ability of most people who have gone to reputable schools to be atrocious. What's worse, they're ignorant about their ignorance."

For a very long time the deficiencies of college students have been laid at the door of the secondary schools. But here, and in similar pieces

I have read, blame is given to the colleges, even the best of them. And what is most faulted is the colleges' failure to educate students in the most essential subject matters and skills. Such a lack of confidence is surely what the liberal arts college can least stand. But it has been developing steadily over the last three decades, as colleges, following the example of the universities, have increasingly denied any responsibility to prepare students for responsible citizenship and for service to the larger world. Ironically, even as the public looks to higher education to provide the diplomas and certificates necessary to white-collar employment, colleges and universities no longer enjoy the public trust once generously granted them. Indeed, many an observer has alleged that the gulf between town and gown has never been wider than it is today.

The liberal arts college is indeed beleaguered. My anxiety about the future of liberal education has walked these pages, and my hope for its survival rests with the continuing health of the small private college; the university's priorities will guarantee its continuing neglect of undergraduate education. I am sadly aware that many alumni, and others who have no direct stake in the survival of the liberal arts college, fear that in its compromising, its lack of rigor, and its abandoning vital tradition, it has sold its soul in order to enjoy an enhanced life. In face of all the uncertainties and doubts about the viability of the private college, I would urge trustees, presidents, and faculties to consider that the best response they can make to such doubt is to say that they will work to return their college to what it was: an institution devoted to the essential studies and to the moral purposes of liberal education.

Chapter XI
The Once and Future College

My first consultancy, one which taught me more than any other, was not under the aegis of the National Endowment for the Humanities. It was at a Michigan college affiliated with the Reformed Church, a member of the consortium to which Kenyon belonged. In 1965 its dean asked me to evaluate the freshman/sophomore year programs there, for he and his colleagues had grown anxious about their losing large numbers of students at the end of the second year. I accepted readily; it would give me an opportunity to see the workings of another college (I was still only in my second year as Kenyon's Dean).

Over several days on the campus I sat in on courses that were typically taken by students who were satisfying curricular requirements: introductory courses in the humanities, sciences, social sciences. But I learned little there which would explain student departures. My interviews with students and faculty members, however, quickly proved enlightening. Students were frank to say that they were transferring to the University of Michigan or to Michigan State because, by the end of the sophomore year, they would have their "liberal education" behind them and would find stronger major programs at the university. They understood liberal education to be simply the sampling of the subject matters they were getting through distribution requirements, courses that would give them the "breadth" they imagined was all there was to liberal education. They had not understood any relationship between those "breadth" courses and the work they would undertake in a major program, beyond what some thought of as the acquisition of certain skills that would be useful in their upper-class years. Nor had they seen any linkages between the subject matters of their courses, any crossovers of interests or questions. Each course remained for them isolated from the others, really intended, as they saw it, to give them an introduction to the work of departments so that they could eventually choose one as a major. At best they thought of their first two college years as a backdrop to the serious work they would undertake at the university, perhaps some information acquired which they could draw on at a later stage.

Like students in many a college, those students used the word "major" as though it meant the "only" or "exclusive" interest; they did not understand that "major" implied the existence of "minor" or "other" interests that should complement their major study. When I asked them what might convince them to stay on and graduate, some said the college's strong ties to their church, while others said the wish to work with a particular professor they had come to respect. But a sadly large number could find no reason to stay on; they would take with them what they imagined they had come for.

Later in the week I heard faculty members talking of students "getting out of the way" the very courses the students understood to be liberal education, so that they could get on to "serious work." (I would hear like statements at many colleges in later years.) For those faculty members, clearly, the only serious work being done in their institution was work in the courses in their major programs, the very programs the students thought not strong enough to hold them at the college, while the "breadth" courses were "serious" only to the extent that they served students as the introduction to their major. In fact, those courses were designed from the beginning with an eye to their being the introductory course to the major, not for the students for whom this would likely be the only encounter they would ever have with that discipline. A member of the science division said emphatically to me, "The only way to understand science is to do science." Substitute "history," "philosophy," "political science," "sociology," or what have you for "science" in that statement and you have explanation for much student dissatisfaction with "breadth" courses. Such assumptions readily convince students that, if they are not going to "do" that particular discipline, they might as well close their minds to it forever.

Neither among the college's students nor its professors did I find people talking of synthesizing knowledge or integrating subject matters. To the extent that the college was expecting its students to be liberally educated, it was relying completely on juxtaposition. Some of the bright youngsters I talked to that week were making connections for themselves, finding it interesting that X in this course was challenged or illuminated by Y in that, but such discoveries were, as nearly as I could tell, always their own. I heard nothing in the classes I audited to suggest a conscious effort on the part of professors to point to larger contexts or interdependencies. Subject matters were being dealt with in isolation from others.

Years later a professor of economics at Kenyon told me what brought him to recognize just how capable of compartmentalizing their knowledge students are. He was attracted into auditing an ecology course in the biology department, taught by a professor who had won a student following for his vigorous defense of wetlands and other threatened environments. My colleague recognized in the class several economics majors, who dutifully took notes and, to judge by the discussion that followed on the lecture, embraced altogether the arguments the ecologist had advanced for guarding those environments against any and all comers. Later my colleague asked those students why they had not questioned the professor about a matter that should have been obvious to students of economics: the opportunity costs that inevitably figure in such an issue. The students confessed that they had thought "opportunity costs" were something they dealt with only in economics courses.

My Michigan college, I was to conclude, was relying completely on the Reformed Church and Dutch ethnicity to create a sense of corporate identity and membership. Those were not enough to persuade the departing sophomores that they should stay for four years. With his faculty colleagues, the dean had accepted the common student explanation for leaving: it would be cheaper for them by far to be at the public university for their junior and senior years. The students didn't want to hurt their professors' feelings by telling them the truth they had been willing to tell me, the outsider.

I would come to call what I found in that first consultancy and later at other colleges the "inverted T of undergraduate education": two years of spreading the student across a "breadth" of disciplines followed by two years of "depth," meaning the student's concentration on a single department's work. "Depth and breadth" were simply juxtaposed like "land and sea," "town and country," separate identities not achieving a union.

(I find now a distressing counterpart to that problem, which poses a significant threat to the independent college. Increasing numbers of students, following the advice of high school guidance counselors or the urging of financially-stressed parents, are taking their first two years at the local community college, transferring then to a four-year institution. Such students have told me that the arrangement gives them the least expensive degree they can obtain and, like those Michigan students, they view the undergraduate years as readily divisible into two unrelated halves.)

The uneducated or illiberally educated person speaks, when making an assertion, either out of sadly limited knowledge or with the conviction that allows for no other understanding. Liberal education has always set itself against such narrowness and dogmatism. In a college that chooses to call itself a liberal arts college, then, we must expect a concern to have students earn a fuller understanding than any single academic division can provide and to be able to accomplish a synthesizing of the knowledge they have gained in a major program and outside it. We must wish to see them achieve a coherent organizing of their academic experience into an intelligible and persuasive whole that is more than the sum of its parts.

We can readily acknowledge that in most of the colleges which say they are colleges of the liberal arts, work is going on which purists would declare is not truly liberal. That is to say, such work is clearly pre-professional or straightforwardly training in particular skills. We can easily challenge the claim of any such critic that his own institution is "pure liberal arts," for it would be impossible to find today a college in which there is no pre-professional activity going on. The English major who takes seminars on critical theory rather than on literary texts is engaging in pre-professional study, as is the history major who takes a course on "The Practice and Theory of History." To be sure, English and history are liberal arts, as accounting is certainly not. Faculty prejudice against the business community may keep business courses out of a college's offerings, but it isn't much of a step, surely, from having a department of education, with a curriculum largely dictated by powers outside the college, to having business administration. Training in necessary skills, too, has its place, particularly now when many students will not have acquired them in high school. In every discipline there is a need for certain skills to be mastered; not for nothing were first courses in English departments called "Reading and Writing," those having always been the essential tools for work in the humanities, if not in all the liberal arts. Such skill courses, which today surely include the first course or two in computer science, are necessary to the contemporary liberal arts college. They should not be scorned.

In truth, most contemporary colleges could be called "liberal arts plus," for in virtually every one of them work is offered that would not have fitted into the "essential studies" Gordon Chalmers described. In any college today the largest number of students will be preparing for careers in business; where business administration is taught, about half the juniors and seniors will be majoring in business. In other colleges they will likely be concentrating in economics or even a pre-business major analogous to the pre-med and pre-law programs that have long existed even in the purest of the pure colleges. In the majority of liberal arts colleges, again, there will be a flourishing department of education, preparing students for careers in teaching. Still others may have a music conservatory, a nursing program, programs in minority or international studies which fall outside the traditional framework. In some departments there will be such a continuing emphasis on marketable skills that it would be impossible to call them "liberal studies." But I shall not wish to say that they should be excluded from the colleges of the liberal arts; they may be necessary to their survival. But it is crucial that the essential studies flourish alongside them.

The obligation of the college that calls itself a liberal arts college is to ensure, through its curriculum and graduation requirements, that every student understand what makes education liberal rather than illiberal, what distinguishes education from training, and what are the characteristics of the liberally educated person. (As attentively as students may listen to the president or the academic dean address them on liberal education, they will not be convinced if the rhetoric does not speak to what goes on in the classroom; it is from their professors that students do learn, finally.) Further, the college should provide a program of study in which a necessary comprehensive academic experience is balanced by depth of understanding in one liberal discipline. It should ensure that the program of study is organized in such a way that the student working in a major program always feels the tug of other modes of inquiry. For the pre-professional major, then, that would require a strong minor in a liberal discipline; the business administration major might have a minor in English or history, say. The college must set limits on how much credit towards the degree can be earned in a single discipline so that the student is never able to shut himself off from other concerns. The college must also wish to ensure that breadth of interest is associated not only with the first two years or with introductory courses in departments; it will seek to have its students see the four undergraduate years as a unit, necessarily subdivided into manageable parts, but still a whole that is to be comprehended.

The first rule for the work of the liberal arts college must be that it will never waste the student's time. There is so much to be mastered in the four years that the student's precious time must be given to what is central. The peripheral may be interesting to those who have already commanded the center, but the undergraduate course should always be focused upon the best and the most enlightening the discipline can offer. The college that chooses to offer "The History of Baseball" alongside "The History of the United States since 1919" and for the same amount of academic credit is failing to give its students appropriate guidance and a sense of priority.

How utterly wrong for the college is the practice of describing academic work in terms of "credit hours," as though learning were simply a matter of accumulating time in classrooms. What nonsense to grant five hours of credit for an introductory language course where most of the work is done in the classroom, as against only two for an advanced seminar because the students spend just two hours face to face with their professor and do a lot of private study. How contrary to the very idea of education it is to invite students to think in terms of the smallest units.

If liberal education, understood in the terms I have described, is to be reinstated in our colleges, the colleges will have to have strong leadership. The history of Kenyon College in the twentieth century gives ample evidence of the need for strong and *continuing* leadership; Kenyon's best years were in times when it was well led, its lesser years when its presidents and academic officers were either weak or put other priorities before their responsibility to liberal education. But leadership must begin with the trustees, for theirs is the power and responsibility to determine what shall be the character of the college they are pledged to serve. To them now must come a call like that Martin Luther delivered to the princes and city councilors of his time: that they commit to liberal education. Too often trustees have thought their interest extended only to the budget and the state of the campus buildings. Too often they have deferred to presidents and faculties on the matters which truly shape the institution's life.

The best statement I know on collegiate governance is that published by the American Association of University Professors, which clearly distinguishes the authorities and responsibilities of the faculty (those appointed to teach and do research), and the administration (those appointed to carry out the purposes and instructions of the trustees). The AAUP paper leaves no doubt about the ultimate authority being that of the trustees; both by charter and traditional practice a college's trustees are entrusted with determining what shall be the mission of the institution. Too often a faculty committee has been entrusted with the task of defining the mission in a statement for the college catalogue. Most often the paragraphs produced could be accepted by any state university in the country; they are likely to be a prescription for preparing the future graduate student. Trustees must know what they wish their college to stand for and they must articulate it. It is very unlikely today that a private college, unless it be very wealthy, will be able to have an academic leader in the president's office, so vastly altered are the tasks and responsibilities of that position. One reason for the all too rapid turnover in presidencies—the average tenure, I am told, is now about five years—is surely the problem the president has in seeking to reconcile the very different aspects of his or her job. Ask on virtually any campus what faculty, students, administrators, and trustees think is the first task of the president and the answer will be "raising money." For the hard-pressed college, raising money is nearly a full-time job, so great are the needs of the college that wishes to be competitive. Sad to say, the task cannot be given over to development officers, for the alumni, the foundations, the government agencies, and the major donors all expect to see the president face to face. To succeed in that crucial activity the president must, of course, be able to describe persuasively what his college stands for and is doing; he must be the college's first public relations voice. Then there falls to the president the development and management of budgets, the planning of new buildings and the renovation of old. There is a "town-gown" relationship to be handled; working with state agencies and academic consortia; there are consortium or athletic conference meetings, as well as conventions of national organizations. And, of course, supervision of the key staff members and interviewing of candidates for positions. There is travel, travel, travel. It goes on and on .... The first thing I had to do when I became a president was to give up reading the journals of my academic discipline; the *Chronicle of Higher Education* and the *Wall Street Journal* took their place. Many a college by now has understandably decided that its president should be a former development officer, an attorney, a retired general, a business manager; the academic dean is no longer a likely choice. Academic leadership today, I believe, must come from the chief academic officer, sometimes called vice president, sometimes dean of the college, sometimes provost, the title I will use here. The provost should be the equal of the president in one regard: his decisions should stand unless overruled by the trustees. The provost should, of course, be appointed by the president and report to him; he will be the institution's second ranking administrator and be acting president in the president's extended absence. The first responsibility of the provost will be the recruitment and development of the faculty, with the decisions on reappointment, promotion, and tenure being his recommendations to the governing board. If there is a faculty committee on these matters, it must only be advisory; faculty committees do not like to make the tough calls. The provost should accompany the department chair to the national convention that is a first recruiting ground in most instances, deciding which candidates shall be brought to the campus for interview. It will be the provost's task to watch over the curriculum, to ensure that courses have been approved by the full faculty before they are taught, to see to it that courses are well taught. Much of the provost's time, obviously, will be given to evaluation: of professors in their classrooms, of their scholarly work and their participation in the life of the college. In these crucial activities he will be assisted by department heads, for I would have the chairmanship of the department once again be a leadership position, with the chair serving so long as he is promoting the college's interests through the department. The evidence shows by now that a provost cannot provide academic direction when he must work with all the faculty at once through committees, even as the evidence shows that a department will be at peace and its morale high when it has effective leadership from a continuing chair.

"Faculty development" in the liberal arts college cannot mean what it means in the university, namely only the ongoing refinement of the professor's specialty. It must intend the development of the professor's capacity to do the college's work, which will, of course, be first the teaching of his or her discipline. But it will mean also mean the growth into a sense of membership in the college and not only the department. To that end the college should invest funds in summer programs of the kind the Lilly Endowment enabled Kenyon to have in the 'seventies. For it is again clear in the AAUP statement on institutional governance that the faculty are to consider themselves members of the college, their teaching role to be within the framework of the college's mission as established by the governing board. The AAUP text clearly establishes the authority of the faculty over the curriculum: what courses shall be taught and who shall teach them. But that does not grant the faculty authority to introduce courses which are clearly at odds with the college's purpose or to decide to add a new department. Faculty members who cannot agree to do the work of the college should think themselves morally obliged not to accept appointment. I have rejoiced to hear that there are young faculty members in increasing numbers who wish to take teaching seriously and to have a sense of collegiate membership, even as they wish to go on with work in their field. It is they who must be identified and vigorously recruited for the liberal arts college, as Gordon Chalmers well knew fifty years ago; there are plenty of places in the universities for those who wish to be independent contractors.

The essential college needs the devotion of all its members, students, faculty, administrators alike. It should seek constantly to express its corporate identity through activities that bring its members together in the college's name. In many a college these days only athletic events perform that function; weekly assemblies with an address by a visitor or a member of the college are a better answer. The college needs, too, to bring to its assemblies two kinds of persons who can help to shape students: the first, graduates of the institution who can speak cogently about the place of liberal education in their lives, both professional and private; the second, persons with national reputations in the liberal arts who can put the college's work into the largest of contexts. The college can further its own interests appropriately by organizing conferences of the Chalmers and Horwitz kind, which will both give the college needed publicity and bring before the college in a persuasive way the world in which students will eventually find their place. It will be a continuing reminder that the college is seeking to prepare students to be leaders in that world.

I have made plain here my belief that the liberal arts college must once again speak of and celebrate values and I know that is a notion which makes some faculty members nervous. They seem to fear that piety will be made a substitute for scholarship, or that they will be called on to be propagandists for a particular religious faith, to be preachers and not teachers. Some are made uncomfortable by the proposal that belief can be critically examined, though most faculty members in fact spend their working days looking critically at beliefs, whether in a scientific theory, an economic system, or the worth of this or that idea. Whenever I think of teaching values or critically examining belief, I recall one of Kenyon's best undergraduates telling me years ago that when Professor Sutcliffe taught *Paradise Lost* in freshman English, he taught it *reverently*; the freshman thought Sutcliffe must be very devout. Now I knew Sutcliffe to be devoutly agnostic, one who believed neither in Milton's God nor his Satan. But I knew, too, that Sutcliffe revered works of literature and did his best to do justice to the authors' beliefs he found in their works. He argued for the place of *Paradise Lost* in the course, not because he wished to impose Milton's beliefs upon students, but because he thought that poem a seminal statement, one that every student in the humanities should know and value and even revere.

Thoughtful men and women do not espouse values because these have been preached to them, although their first encounter with them may have been in some form of preaching—from their parents, a minister, an author. Rather, they embrace them after considering alternatives, persuaded by them after critical examination of their claim. What we accept as a value represents the tension between our self-interest and another's. A widely embraced value is the correspondence of many interests, an acknowledgement of the surmounting of many selves. Such values may be proposed in the undergraduate curriculum where collegiate education, genuinely conceived and practiced, will demonstrate how extravagant self-interest is challenged and may be redeemed through liberal education. That will require students to examine large communal interests and beliefs. To those interests, then, self-interest, whether it be the student's or that of the discipline, must be actively related if a sense of collegiate values is to emerge. It is the ignoring of those communal interests, in consequence of faculty specialization and exaggerated departmentalism, which has so often made undergraduate education a celebration of narrow self-interest and has made the university mode narcissistic.

The capacity of the essential college to do the work I have proposed will depend, clearly, upon its being able to staff its courses with faculty members who are able to honor both the values of their disciplines and those of the college. That is, to ask of them no more than that they be simultaneously private persons and citizens. It is not to require them to be churchgoers; it is certainly not to ask them to preach. What we may expect from all members of the college's faculty is their thoughtful recognition of the moral dimensions of their work and their sensitivity to students' beliefs. We should wish to find in them loyalty to collegiate purpose and respect for their colleagues in other disciplines. That is simply to expect them to be members of the college—the *collegium*—as well as members of their departments.

The choice for our independent colleges is clear. Either they can be content to take a comfortable and uncontroversial path and train academic technicians, as so many now are doing, or they can be what Thomas Jefferson would have had them be: liberating colleges that work to free students of their provincial limitations and to educate them to the fullness of their humanity. I am well persuaded that trustees and faculties who seek that latter identity for their colleges will have a host of grateful parents choosing to have their children educated in them. *For this is emphatically what the university cannot do. This is how the independent college can be a true alternative.* If the colleges do not choose the latter role they will wither, and both their leaders and our nation will awaken only too late to what has been lost.

Chapter XII
A Curriculum for the Essential College

I have emphasized again and again that in that triangulation of student/subject matter/teacher within which education is accomplished, the crucial element is the teacher. The selection and care of faculty members must be the college's first priority. But the choice of subject matter is nearly as important, and it is to the subject matters of the liberal curriculum that I shall now turn. I wish to propose a specific curriculum design in order that I may give the clearest account possible of what I believe should go into the liberal education of today's American students.

We forget too often when we talk of undergraduate education that students will eventually spend as much time away from their workaday life as they will in it. So much emphasis is placed, when graduation requirements are discussed, on what the student will *do* after graduation that there is little attention given to what the student will *be*. Though liberal education certainly develops skills and knowledge that will be valuable in the world of work—clarity of thought, the ability to analyze and synthesize material, skills in reading and writing—it will just as much develop capacities and understanding that will enlarge a person's ability to live and experience richly. Refinement of mind, development of taste and discrimination, a moral sense, a respect for the different—these are qualities which the study of the liberal arts has been known to develop in students. But, it must be emphasized, whether or not students will reap this harvest will depend on how subject matters are taught. The study of literature can be made as illiberal as any course in a vocational curriculum. When history becomes antiquarianism it ceases to be liberal. When political science is translated into the study of voting patterns of Chicago suburban housewives, it is no longer a liberal art. It is with that caution that any curriculum design must be approached.

Mine is a curriculum for four years of serious work, one that can be successfully attempted, I am confident, by any student admitted to a liberal arts college. I use "curriculum" in its traditional meaning of "a course of study," charted purposefully, with a design over the four years. The four years are necessarily subdivided into operating units, the first being the academic year, the last the course. I wish it were possible to have no other subdivisions, with an academic year that ran from September to June with periodic vacation breaks but with no semesters, terms, or quarters, for I would wish to see students encouraged from the outset to think in terms of the largest units possible. Such a system, in my experience, affords more flexibility in organizing work than any other. But the semester is so established that I cannot here challenge it. However, I would encourage, wherever possible, the organization of work in year-long courses and I shall propose that most of the required courses in my curriculum be such. I shall also retain the traditional sequence of freshman, sophomore, junior, and senior years, expecting that the work of the upper-class years build on what has gone before, the senior year providing a culminating point in both the student's major program and the required general education courses. I also assume that the student will be able to deal with increasingly difficult and larger quantities of work as he or she moves up through the years. The process of liberal education will be understood to go on throughout the four years, with the general education courses providing the vital, continuing context for all other work undertaken and with the faculty referring frequently in their courses to that larger context, so that professors and students alike will grasp the interrelatedness of the curriculum's constituent parts. I wish to ensure that there will never be a sense of topics or questions in isolation.

Certain basic courses are required of all students. There is a value to such requirements, first because the balancing of required courses and electives provides a paradigm for our larger society; our freedom of choice depends on our living within the requirements, the laws that govern us all. Second, they provide the common experience and shared understanding that are essential to a sense of community.

The requirements for graduation are four years of satisfactory course work in which the student earns sixteen units of credit, four units a year. The year's work will be in courses with a value of one unit or one-half (for a semester-long course), as determined first by the department and the provost, and then by the whole faculty. The sixteen units will be earned in this fashion: five and a half in the general education courses required of all students, up to six and a half in the student's major program (including the introductory course), at least four in courses elected by the student with the approval of his or her advisor. Specifically then, in the freshman year the two required basic courses and two units earned in courses in at least two departments; in the sophomore year the two required basic courses and two units in at least two departments; in the junior year the required basic course, two units in the major program, and one unit in one or two other departments; in the senior year the required basic course (taken in either semester), the senior exercise (in either semester), and three other units.

The work of the basic courses is intended to have students understand and celebrate the constitutional liberties of this country and the responsibilities of our citizenship; they should know what it means to be a free American in this age. The courses will demonstrate the other interests against which every student must measure his own. They will employ the different modes of thought and inquiry through which these questions can be approached, as well as the skills needed to deal with them successfully. Students will come to understand that these are questions that eventually call on them to choose the better or worse part and which thus have a moral dimension that cannot be set aside. They will be led, finally, to see that their beliefs and convictions must be examined and evaluated, and ultimately defended.

The basic courses required of all students will be organized in sections, all using the same texts and teaching schedule, so that there will be a campus-wide engagement with a body of work over the four years. That, I believe, can greatly profit a college in achieving an identity and a sense of collegiate purpose.

Below I use Roman numerals to identify the year, capital letters to distinguish the different courses of the year.

IA. *Language and Literature.* (Year-long course.) We begin with language, the fundamentally human activity, which defines our individual experience and permits us to share in the experience of others. Our language joins us to all others who use it and who have ever used it; it is our heritage and the prime bearer of our culture. The effective use of language is the most important skill required in liberal education and a worthy life. Literature is the art form that gives us the most direct access to our common humanity and to the best that humanity has imagined about itself and the world. Ordinarily this course will be taught by members of the English department, though members of other departments might well participate. Texts will be selected for what they let us learn of the human condition everywhere; thus readings should include works in translation from literatures other than English. Regular paper writing will be in response to the works read, with students encouraged to write on matters which link the several works together.

IB. *The political, social, and cultural history of the United States since 1776.* (Year-long course.) This course is not intended to survey every moment in our nation's history! I have audited courses called "Western Civilization" which were marred by their designers' insistence on trying to mention every name, cover every imaginable topic, and catalog every achievement, with the result being a confusing blur for the students. My course would select a half-dozen important periods or topics, say, spending four or five weeks on each so that students have some deep understanding of their significance in shaping our nation. For me an obvious beginning would be the Constitution, a second the Civil War, another slavery and the Civil Rights Movement. Throughout, the course should have "liberty" as its theme; it should celebrate the vision of America that has inspired so many the world over. It is a course that invites the participation of many social scientists as well as other members of the faculty who could contribute guest lectures.

IIA. *The physical universe and its life forms.* (Year-long course.) To create this course is a challenge. It is clearly needed to establish the large context in which our human society functions. It is needed also so that students may understand what science and scientists are actually doing. A scientist friend of mine argues that nothing is more important in undergraduate education than that students come to understand science—so that they can control the scientists. His point is well taken. Members of science departments have usually not been interested in developing courses for students outside their division. Some have spoken scornfully of "bio for poets" and insisted that an understanding of science comes only with taking regular courses in science. But I have talked to many students over the years whose colleges required them to take conventional science courses to satisfy distribution requirements, and in nearly every instance those students had not acquired the understanding the framers of the degree requirements had imagined. In fact, most were resolved to close their minds to science forever. We must acknowledge that there are people—I am one of them—who cannot "do" science, but who wish to understand science and scientists. I am grateful that Kenyon gave me colleagues from whom I was able to learn what my formal education had not provided me; now I read about science and I am able to understand what I read. I want students to be able to read in an informed way about what scientists are doing or failing to do. We urgently need informed public opinion on questions like stem cell research and cloning. We need understanding of all that is involved in proposed exploration of space—including the opportunity costs! The liberal arts college must seek to have on its faculty persons who believe in the need for scientists to reach out across the gulf between the science building and the rest of the campus.

IIB. *The Arts: Responses to the Human Condition.* (Year-long course.) The course might well consider at its beginning the statements of two well-known artists: Picasso's "Art is a lie through which we see the truth," and Warhol's "A work of art is something created by somebody who calls himself an artist." My wish is to have students consider the ways in which people have used the arts to give form to the chaos in the world and their experience of it. They should see the power of the creative imagination and the wresting of beauty out of life's raw materials. They should attempt creative work themselves, whether in the art studio, in writing poetry, in composing a musical work. Is art the universal access to a truth beyond the appearance, as Picasso believed? Or is it only the subjective activity of an individual who seeks nothing beyond his own expression? Does art have a moral dimension? Is art a mirror, a distorting mirror, a window on the world, a dangerous illusion?

III. *Another Culture.* (Year-long course.) This course is deliberately postponed to the junior year, so that students who have come to terms with their own culture may study another. That they should undertake such a study is obvious. Other cultures *demand* our interest and understanding today, but a college cannot possibly address them all. However, the deep study of a second culture will sensitize students to other cultures and give them the means to study them and appreciate their worth. It will broaden the context of what students understand as "the human" as well as help them understand the values and the limits of the forms of our own society. The particular college's resources will determine what it can do in this course and here there is room for a variety of disciplines which can serve: political science, Classics, anthropology, history, religion, foreign language and literature departments might all contribute a year-long course or even a pairing of semester courses. In a very small college the second culture might have to be European, but it would obviously be better if the student were to study a culture outside that frame. (What I would not admit under this rubric is the conventional foreign language requirement. I am a foe of such requirements and I say so believing that I must have listened to every argument, pro and con, that can possibly be advanced in discussion of them. Most often, faculties vote for a language requirement in the belief that students will thereby apprehend a second culture—in two, three, or four semesters! No, they will not. The sad truth is that elementary and intermediate language courses, for the vast majority of students, are a waste of valuable time. Colleges ought to expect, indeed require, that their entering students will have had at least two years of a foreign language; they ought to join the universities in demanding of the secondary schools that they offer four consecutive years of foreign language instruction.)

IV. *Ethics and Belief.* (Semester course.) This capstone of the general education courses would require students to look back over the courses they have taken and consider what the moral dimensions of their studies are. They should also consider their beliefs—political, social, economic, religious—and examine them with the same careful scrutiny they have brought to their studies to this point. To be truly liberating, undergraduate education must bring students to understand that all they have learned should be brought into a coherent set of beliefs; they will spend their lives acting on beliefs, knowingly or unknowingly. Though professors of philosophy, religion, or literature are the most likely persons to conduct this course, faculty members from other disciplines might welcome the opportunity to test themselves in it. The course should be embraced by the whole faculty as evidence that their college stands for education rather than training, for the pursuit of knowledge to humane ends.

Course IV has a counterpart in the student's senior year in what I will call "the senior exercise," a title that will permit departments to make a capstone to the student's major program in whatever form best suits their work. In one department it might be a thesis, in another a series of papers, in a third a series of experiments, all of them having in common the expectation that the student will demonstrate convincingly a capacity to work independently and rigorously.

No curriculum, no set of degree requirements, no institutional statement of purpose can guarantee that a student will be liberally educated. The magic of Thomas Mann's mountain is not available to those who seek only entertainment or the feeding of their appetites. It works for Hans Castorp because *he* works, because he opens himself to influences and experiences, because he attends critically to those who wish to teach him, because he seeks a truth that will illuminate his world and guide his life, and not the least, because he learns what love requires. My curriculum can grant students what Cardinal Newman called "the power of viewing many things at once as one whole, of referring them severally to their true place in the universal system, of understanding their respective values, and determining their mutual dependence." It will bring them to understand that knowledge does not come out of a random association of ideas or the isolation of a question from others. The process of the curriculum in the whole will have students recognize the hazards of ignorance and lead them to make wise decisions in all aspects of learning—and of life. Most importantly, its senior year components will bring them to understand that the ultimate purpose of liberal education is, in

President Chalmers's phrase, "commitment and action," the moral uses of knowledge.

It is with Gordon Chalmers that I end, as I began with him, sharing his faith that America's students can rise to the challenge of the liberal curriculum: "From direct experience with youth of almost all types and in almost all social conditions I know for a fact that the plain American boy and girl are capable of dealing actively with some of the ideas men live by."

The Essential College

Acknowledgements

Many colleagues and friends have contributed to this book, directly or indirectly, and I am grateful to them. I wish to particularly thank Jeremy McNamara, Kenyon '53, and William Urban of Monmouth College for their advice and encouragement. P.F. Kluge, writer in residence at Kenyon, has graciously permitted me to quote from his interview of President Jordan. I am especially indebted to Charles E. Rice of Kenyon College, with whom I have discussed undergraduate education for over fifty years, always to my profit.